Italian
Wine & Cheese
Made Simple

Second Edition

Praise for Italian & Cheese Made Simple

"The second edition of Italian Wine & Cheese Made Simple is the perfect book for anyone who is an Italian Wine & Cheese lover. Bob & Gary's books have a unique down-to-earth approach that experts and novices alike can enjoy." *Giovanni Bertani –Tenuta Santa Maria alla Pieve Winery, Veneto, Italy www.tenutapieve.com*

"So many cheeses, so many decisions... Bob & Gary's book takes the pain out of making that perfect pairing decision!" *Lisa Griffiths, Director of Sales & Marketing– igourmet.com Cheese Selections*

...Another great book from Gary and Bob! "It's amazing how they make it so easy for anyone to fall in love with the world of Italian wine and cheese." *Massimiliano Giacomini, Export Manager, Ferrari Trento, Italy www.cantineferrari.it*

"Bravo! What a novel approach to the difficulties of cheese and wine pairing. I especially like the helpful charts." *Mario Di Chiara Owner/ Executive Chef IL Poeta Italian Restaurant, New York*

"Expert or beginner, Italian Wine & Cheese Made Simple or Italian Wine Notes is a must for everyone." *Tom McLoone, Beverage Director of Club Metropolitan, N.Y.C.*

"A book no one should be without—a must for anyone who shops for and enjoys Italian cheese and wine." *Dave Trieger / Vigna Uva Vino www.vignauvavino.blogspot.com*

"Gary and Bob's book is a unique guide to the world of Italian wine and cheeses. Every time we pick a new wine or cheese for our wine bar, we measure it to Gary and Bob's standard" *Ollie Sakhno, Keuka Kafe, A Wine Bar, Forest Hills, New York*

Front cover design by Gary Grunner and David Trieger

Front cover photography
By Gary Grunner, Copyright 2015

Italian Wine Map created by Corey Bippes of Sundancer Graphics, Inc.
www.sundancergraphics.com

Contact Information:

Gary Grunner
E-Mail:
garyrgrunner@aol.com
gary@grapesonthego.com

Bob Lipinski
E-mail: bob@hibs-usa.com

Italian
Wine & Cheese
Made Simple

Second Edition

Bob Lipinski & Gary Grunner

BOB LIPINSKI

Dedication

This book is dedicated to my family:
my two sons, John and Matt,
and especially my loving and special wife Kathie,
for without her support, love,
dedication, loyalty, and understanding
…you wouldn't be reading this book.

GARY GRUNNER

Dedication

This Book is dedicated to my wife Carolina
and my two sons Dave and Max

Acknowledgments

To all the wonderful wineries, winemakers, cheese producers, wine salesmen, sommeliers, restaurant owners, and fine wine shop retailers who shared their passion and knowledge with us over the years, we thank you. This career is not as easy as it looks from the outside, but together we built one of the greatest industries filled with wonderful loyal friends **and yes a few major #@%#@ but there was always a glass of wine paired with a dish of wonderful cheeses to brighten up your day!**

TABLE OF CONTENTS

"Italian Wine & Cheese Made Simple"

Preface

THOSE OF US who enjoy cheese and wine, whether serving them before dinner as appetizers, during parties or just for a casual snack, drink or gathering will spend hours reading the many cheeses and wines described. Unfortunately, in today's world, a person who enjoys a certain cheese (e.g. a "Fontina" from Italy) often has difficulty in finding a suitable wine to serve with it. At the opposite end of the spectrum, a person with a fine bottle of "Sangiovese" from Italy looks for the perfect matching cheese, many times without success. Oftentimes, one finds that when certain wines and cheeses are matched together they taste terrible. This is usually due to differences in flavor or the chemical imbalance between the high levels of acid in the wines, and the alkaline levels in the cheeses. This book eliminates "mismatching" by carefully selecting the wines and cheeses that **do** enhance each other.

The first chapter of the book describes the cheese with appropriate wine selections; while the second chapter reverses this...the wines are described with appropriate cheese selections. Therefore, that cheese lover (*turophile*) can pick out their favorite cheese, then turn to **Chapter 1** and find a list of suggested wines. While in a wine shop, a consumer can select their favorite Sangiovese, then turn to **Chapter 2** and find a list of suggested cheeses.

The book is divided into Seven Sections

Introduction: Traces the history, background, and origin of cheese as well as where and how it was first made. Through a "time-travel," one can see important dates that helped shape the cheeses we most love.

Listing of PDO Cheeses as of 2015: A list of 51 cheeses that have been awarded the "Protected Designation of Origin" (PDO) designation.

Chapter 1: Cheeses "A to Z"—each alphabetically listed cheese is described by "region of origin," color, size, appearance, taste, and any other pertinent information. Beneath some of the more popular cheese's description will be the recommended beverages. More than 130 cheeses are described.

Chapter 2: Wines "A to Z" (And Other Beverages)—each alphabetically listed wine (or other beverage) is described by country of origin, flavor characteristics, and any other pertinent information. Beneath some of the more popular wine's description will be the recommended cheeses.

Appendix A: Wine (And Other Beverages) & Cheese Recommendations—a list of beverages, with their corresponding cheeses in a simplistic format.

Appendix B: Regions Where Cheese is Made—shows each of Italy's 20 regions with a list of cheeses made there.

Appendix C: Grapes: The Wines They Make (And Other Beverages)—Wines are categorized by grape variety with corresponding wines that they produce. As an example, Sangiovese is the grape used to make Chianti Wine.

Appendix D: Cheese & Fruit Pairing—Presents a cheese with a list of various fruits that pair quite nicely with cheese.

Appendix E: Glossary— A concise list of terms and words most frequently used for making, purchasing or enjoying cheese.

A book of this caliber presents a "ready-reference guide" that can be used repeatedly without ever becoming outdated. Both the novice and expert alike will literally find hundreds of wine and cheese pairings. This book can easily be carried into your favorite cheese or wine shop as an index for pairings.

This book contains more than 130 cheeses in simple, concise terms that describe them, along with wines and fruits they pair with. This book will be very useful in today's market where countless scores of wine and cheese shops, along with wine bars, are constantly opening their doors.

Introduction

THE HAPPIEST MARRIAGE in the world of gastronomy is the mating of cheese and wine. They complement, contrast, and even clash with each other; they agree with the stomach as eagerly as they agree with the palate and offer doubly delicious possibilities for guests.

The making of cheese was a natural consequence of man's ability to procure more milk from his domestic animals than he could consume before it spoiled. Most cheese is made from cow's milk, simply because cows are milked more generally throughout the world than other animals. Smaller quantities are made from the milk of goats and sheep. For ages, man has produced cheese from the milk of buffalo (water), camel, cow, donkey, goat, llama, lion, mare, reindeer, sheep (ewe), sow, tiger, whale, yak, and even a zebu.

Cheese is a method of using milk after it has curdled without missing any of its qualities. It was one of the first foods man was able to conserve and this must surely have been an important discovery. According to archeologists, cheesemaking can be traced back to 6,000 B.C., based on artifacts and pictures on stone tablets in Macedonia, northern Greece. In addition, what appears to be the remains of cheese have been found in Egyptians tombs dating back to 2300 B.C. Early man must have wondered why the stomachs of young goats or lambs contained not milk but a solid, whitish, sweet-smelling mass. Legend has it that the first cheese was made accidentally by a shepherd who carried milk in a leather pouch made from a sheep's stomach. The rennet in the pouch lining, which combined with the sun's heat, caused the milk to separate into curds and whey. He found at nightfall that the whey satisfied his thirst and the cheese (curd) satisfied his hunger and had a delightful flavor. There must have been endless experiments by peasants, monks, and farmers with milk, rennet, and salt until they were able to establish a reliable way of making what we know as cheese.

According to ancient records, cheese was used as a food more than 4,000 years ago. It was made and eaten in Biblical times. Travelers from Asia are believed to have brought the art of cheesemaking to Europe. Cheese was made in many parts of the Roman Empire when it was at its height. Then cheesemaking was introduced to England by the Romans. During the Middle Ages—from the decline of the Roman Empire until the discovery of America—as well as later, cheese was made and improved by the monks in the monasteries of Europe. Gorgonzola was made in the Po Valley in Italy in 879 A. D. and Italy became the cheesemaking center of Europe in the tenth century. The Pilgrims included cheese in the ship's supplies when they made their famous voyage to America in the Mayflower in 1620.

The making of natural cheese is an art centuries old. It consists of separating most of the milk solids from the milk by curdling with rennet or bacterial culture or both and separating the curd from the whey by heating, stirring, and pressing. Most cheeses are made from whole milk. For certain types of cheese both milk and cream are used, and for other types, skim milk, whey or mixtures of these used.

The distinctive flavor and body and texture characteristics of the various cheeses are due to:

1. The kind of milk used
2. The method used for curdling the milk and for cutting, cooking, and forming the curd.
3. The type of bacteria or mold used in ripening
4. The amount of salt or other seasonings added
5. The conditions of ripening such as temperature, humidity, and length of time. Sometimes only minor differences in the procedures followed may make another.

After the cheese has been formed into its characteristic shape it is given a coating of wax or other protective coating or wrapping and allowed to cure or age for varying lengths of time depending upon the kind or variety of cheese being made.

When the cheese has reached its proper curing state it is often cut or sliced from larger blocks or wheels into more suitable sizes for consumer use. The refrigerated showcase in a modern food market is most enticing with its display of various shapes and sizes of cheese packages such as wedges, oblongs, segments, cubes, slices, blocks, and cut portions.

Cheese is a highly nutritious and palatable food. It is of value in the diet because it contains in concentrated form almost all the protein and usually most of the fat, as well as essential minerals, vitamins, and other nutrients, of milk.

Most cheeses are made from cow, goat, or sheep's milk. Here are rough calculations as to the approximate milk yields.

1 cow yields 8 to 20 quarts of milk per day
1 goat yields 3 to 4.5 quarts of milk per day
1 sheep yields about 1 quart of milk per day

Some Dates of Importance...

- **879**: Gorgonzola Cheese was first made in the Po Valley in Italy, and Italy became the cheesemaking center of Europe in the tenth century.

- **1100**: Stracchino, a generic term applied to cheeses, which since around 1100 A.D., have been produced in Italy.

- **1277**: Castelmagno Cheese of Piedmont, Italy was first made.

- **1350**: Caciocavallo Cheese of Italy was first mentioned in a short story by Franco Sacchetti. Supposedly, Caciocavallo got its name because two cheeses are often tied together and hung over a pole, as if astride a horse.

- **1400s**: Mozzarella Cheese dates back to the 1400s in southern Italy.

- **1870**: In the Asiago plateau of Veneto, Italy, Asiago cheese was made for the first time.

- **1877**: Auricchio founded the Auricchio Cheese Company in San Giuseppe Vesuviano, near Naples, Italy. In 1979, Gennaro's great-grandson, Errico Auricchio moved his family to the United States. They settled in Wisconsin for the abundance of top-quality milk. Auricchio is noted for its Provolone cheese.

- **1906**: Bel Paese Cheese was created by Egidio Galbani, an Italian cheesemaker and was named after the title of a children's geography book (published in 1873), written by his close friend, Father Antonio Stoppani. Galbani wanted to make a soft cheese similar to *Saint-Paulin* and after his return from France, created a cheese he named *"Bel Paese."*

- **1939**: Parmigiano-Reggiano Cheese of Italy. The inedible rind that encases the cheese is imprinted with a repeating pattern with the stippled words "Parmigiano-Reggiano," the official title bestowed by governmental decree. In addition to the stippled words, the wheel is branded with the *Tutela Consorzio Parmigiano-Reggiano* oval, which is a quality assurance that the cheese has been produced at government certified dairies in the Parma and Reggio districts of Italy.

- **1941**: Italico, a group of semisoft, delicately-flavored cheeses (Bel Paese and Robiola are examples), which according to a Ministerial Decree, issued by Mussolini on May 10, 1941, required these cheeses to use the name Italico. Now Italico is a recognized cheese in its own right.

- **1977**: A catalogue published listed 451 different Italian cheeses, mostly made in northern Italy. Across the length and breadth of Italy there are many different pastures and methods of cheese making and countless local dishes are made with these various cheeses. As of 2010, more than 600 cheeses have been identified from Italy alone!

Map of Italy

Valle d'Aosta

Lombardy

Trentino-Alto Adige

Friuli-Venezia Giulia

Veneto

Piedmont

Liguria

Emilia-Romagna

Marches

Tuscany

Abruzzo

Umbria

Molise

Rome

Apulia

Latium

Campania

Sardinia

Basilicata

Calabria

Sicily

Listing of PDO Cheeses as of 2015

Protected Designation of Origin (PDO). According to European Union (EU) Law, they protect the names of regional cheeses, their origins, and methods of production. The legislation came into effect in 1992.

Name of Cheese	Year of PDO	Region/s
Asiago d'Allevo	1996	Trentino-Alto Adige, Veneto
Asiago Pressato	1996	Trentino-Alto Adige, Veneto
Bitto	1996	Lombardy
Bra	1996	Piedmont
Caciocavallo Silano	1996	Apulia, Basilicata, Calabria, Campania, Molise
Canestrato Pugliese	1996	Apulia
Casatella Trevigiana	2008	Veneto
Casciotta d'Urbino	1996	Marches
Castelmagno	1996	Piedmont
Fiore Sardo	1996	Sardinia

Fontina	1996	Valle d'Aosta
Formaggella del Luinese	2011	Lombardy
Formaggio di Fossa di Sogliano	2009	Emilia-Romagna, Marches
Formai de Mut dell'Alta Valle Brembana	1996	Lombardy
Gorgonzola	1996	Lombardy, Piedmont
Grana Padano	1996	Emilia-Romagna, Lombardy, Piedmont, Trentino-Alto Adige, Veneto
Montasio	1996	Friuli-Venezia Giulia, Veneto
Monte Veronese	1996	Veneto
Mozzarella di Bufala Campana	1996	Apulia, Campania, Latium, Molise
Murazzano	1996	Piedmont
Nostrano Valtrompia	2012	Lombardy
Parmigiano-Reggiano	1996	Emilia-Romagna, Lombardy
Pecorino Crotonese	2014	Calabria
Pecorino delle Balze Volterrane	2015	Tuscany
Pecorino di Filiano	2007	Basilicata
Pecorino di Picinisco	2013	Latium
Pecorino Romano	1996	Latium, Sardinia, Tuscany
Pecorino Sardo	1996	Sardinia
Pecorino Siciliano	1996	Sicily
Pecorino Toscano	1996	Tuscany
Piacentinu Ennese	2011	Sicily
Piave	2010	Veneto
Primo Sale	1996	Sicily
Provolone del Monaco	2010	Campania
Provolone Valpadana	1996	Emilia-Romagna, Lombardy, Trentino-Alto Adige, Veneto
Puzzone di Moena	2014	Trentino-Alto Adige

Quartirolo Lombardo	1996	Lombardy
Ragusano	1996	Sicily
Raschera	1996	Piedmont
Ricotta di Bufala Campana	2010	Apulia, Campania, Latium, Molise
Ricotta Romana	2005	Latium
Robiola di Roccaverano	1996	Piedmont
Salva Cremasco	2012	Lombardy
Spressa delle Giudicarie	2003	Trentino-Alto Adige
Squacquerone di Romagna	2012	Emilia-Romagna
Stelvio	2007	Trentino-Alto Adige
Taleggio	1996	Lombardy, Piedmont, Veneto
Toma Piemontese	1996	Piedmont
Valle d'Aosta Fromadzo	1996	Valle d'Aosta
Valtellina Casera	1996	Lombardy
Vastedda della Valle del Belice	2010	Sicily

Cheeses A - Z

Letter
A

Abbespata (ah-beh-SPAH-tah) A smoked ricotta, sheep's milk cheese made in the town of Crotone in the region of Calabria.

Acceglio (ah-CHEH-yoh) A small, soft, fresh, and slightly tangy cow's milk cheese made in the province of Cuneo, Piedmont.

Aostino (ah-OH-stee-noh) A soft and buttery textured, mild flavored, cow's milk cheese that has been allowed to sour. It is round with a light yellow interior, few large holes and after additional two or three months of ripening in salt brine, the cheese has more flavor and is called *Salmistra*. Aostino, made in the region of Valle d'Aosta is a popular dessert cheese frequently eaten with honey and fruits. <u>Recommended Beverages</u>: **Red**: Amarone della Valpolicella, Nebbiolo; **White**: Chenin Blanc; **Other**: Champagne and Sparkling Wines (semisweet to sweet); Madeira (dry); Marsala (dry); Semisweet to Sweet Wines; Vermouth (sweet).

Asiago (ah-see-AH-goh) (***PDO* 1996**)

- _Similar To_: *Goya* (Argentina), *Montasio* (Italy), and *Parmigiano-Reggiano* (when aged)
- _Region of Origin_: Trentino-Alto Adige and Veneto (also made in the United States)
- _History_: Named for the Asiago plateau where the cheese was first made around 1000.
- _Type Of Milk_: Originally from sheep's milk (until 1500s) and was called *Pecorino d'Asiago*. Nowadays cow's milk is used.
- _Appearance And Shape_: Light straw-yellow exterior, with tiny openings; dark inedible rind; wheel-shaped
- _Texture_: Semi-firm to hard; *grana-type* cheese
- _Aroma And Flavor_: Medium sharp to sharp, depending on age; nutty flavor
- _Comments_: Suitable for grating when hard. Other types of Asiago Cheese are Asiago d'Allevo (aged), Asiago Grasso Monte (semisoft), and Asiago Pressato (pressed) (***PDO* 1996**).
- _Recommended Beverages_: **Red** Aglianico, Amarone della Valpolicella, Barbera, Bardolino, Cabernet Sauvignon, Dolcetto, Grignolino, Lambrusco, Malbec, Merlot, Montepulciano d'Abruzzo, Nebbiolo, Petite Sirah, Pinot Noir, Primitivo, Sangiovese, Valpolicella, Zinfandel: **White**: Chardonnay, Cortese, Fiano di Avellino, Friulano, Gewürztraminer, Orvieto, Pinot Grigio, Riesling, Sauvignon Blanc, Trebbiano d'Abruzzo, Verdicchio; **Other**: Champagne and Sparkling Wine (dry); Madeira (dry); Marsala (dry); Port; Sherry (dry); Semisweet to Sweet Wines; Vermouth (sweet); Bourbon and Tennessee Whiskey
- _See_: Grana, Pressato, and Vezzena

Asiago d'Allevo (ah-see-AH-goh dahl-LEH-voh) (***PDO 1996***) A cow's milk cheese with a straw-colored rind and an ivory interior with small regular holes. It is produced in three different stages of aging: *mezzano* (aged more than four months), *vecchio* ("old," aged more ten months) and *stravecchio* (aged more 15 months). *See* Asiago.

B

Bagozzo (bah-GOHZ-tzoh)
- *Also Known As*: *Grana Bagozzo* and *Bresciano* (after the city of Brescia)
- *Similar To*: Parmigiano-Reggiano
- *Region of Origin*: Lombardy
- *History*: First mention of its existence was made in 1500
- *Type Of Milk*: Cow
- *Appearance And Shape*: Whitish-yellow body; the body is sometimes colored red; Small wheels
- *Texture*: Hard
- *Aroma And Flavor*: Sharp
- *Comments*: A grana-type cheese
- *Recommended Beverages*: **Red** Aglianico, Amarone della Valpolicella, Barbera, Bardolino, Cabernet Sauvignon, Dolcetto, Grignolino, Lambrusco, Merlot, Montepulciano d'Abruzzo, Nebbiolo, Petite Sirah, Pinot Noir, Primitivo, Sangiovese, Valpolicella, Zinfandel: **White**: Chardonnay, Cortese, Fiano di Avellino, Friulano, Gewürztraminer, Orvieto, Pinot Grigio, Riesling, Sauvignon Blanc, Trebbiano d'Abruzzo, Verdicchio;

Other: Champagne and Sparkling Wine (dry); Marsala (dry); Port; Sherry (dry); Semisweet to Sweet Wines; Vermouth (sweet); Scotch Whisky; Bourbon and Tennessee Whiskey
- *See*: Grana

Bel Paese (behl pah-EH-zeh)

- *Also Known As*: *Bel Piano Lombardo, Bel Piemonte, Bella Alpina,* and *Bella Milano,* and *Fior d'Alpe*
- *Similar To*: *Atzmon* (Israel) Chantelle (United States), Pastorella del Cerreto di Sorano (Italy), Richelieu (Canada), Saint Stephano (Germany)
- *Region of Origin*: Melzo, Lombardy (also made in the United States)
- *History*: It was created in 1906 by Egidio Galbani, an Italian cheesemaker and was named after the title of a children's geography book (published in 1873), written by his close friend, Father Antonio Stoppani. Galbani wanted to make a soft cheese similar to *Saint-Paulin* and after his return from France, created a cheese he named *Bel Paese* (beautiful country).
- *Type Of Milk*: Cow
- *Appearance And Shape*: Slightly gray exterior; rindless; creamy yellow interior. Familiar chipboard box showing the map of Italy with Melzo, the little town near Milan where Bel Paese is made, in beige and pale green, with a picture of Antonio Stoppani, a priest; Cylindrical-shaped
- *Texture*: Semisoft, smooth, and buttery
- *Aroma And Flavor*: Mild to moderately robust; delicately tart, tangy, lightly salty, and fruity
- *Comments*: The name Bel Paese translated means "beautiful country"
- *Recommended Beverages*: **Red**: Barbera, Bardolino, Beaujolais, Merlot, Petite Sirah, Pinot Noir, Sangiovese, Valpolicella, Zinfandel; **White**: Chardonnay, Chenin Blanc, Frascati,

Orvieto, Pinot Grigio, Riesling, Sauvignon Blanc, Soave, Verdicchio; **Other**: Port; Sherry (semisweet)
- _See_: Italico

Bernardo (behr-NAHR-doh) A cow's (sometimes goat's milk added) milk cheese from the region of Lombardy. It is cylindrical in shape with a yellow-brown exterior due to the addition of saffron. Its interior is ivory-colored colored with a few holes, and a mild and pleasant flavor. Also known as _Formaggella Bernarda_ or _Bernarde_. Recommended Beverages: Friulano, Gewürztraminer, Pinot Bianco, Pinot Grigio, and dry Sherry.

Bitto (BEE-toh) (*PDO 1996*)
- _Similar To_: Fontina and Montasio
- _Region of Origin_: Valtellina Valley in Lombardy. It owes its name to the Bitto stream in the valley.
- _History_: The cheese has been made since at least the eleventh century
- _Type Of Milk_: Cow (and some goat)
- _Appearance And Shape_: Large holes when young; reducing in size when aged; white to pale straw with a few holes; Many shapes
- _Texture_: Firm and hard
- _Aroma And Flavor_: Sweet, delicate taste; with age it develops a sharper and richer flavor.
- _Comments_: Generally aged up to three years; suitable for grating when hard. Usually sprinkled on top of polenta.
- _Recommended Beverages_: Amarone della Valpolicella, Cortese, Nebbiolo, Orvieto, and Primitivo

Blu del Moncenisio (bloo dehl mohn-CHEH-nee-zio) A cylindrical-shaped, cow's milk (sometimes goat's milk is added) blue cheese made in Piedmont. It has white or straw-colored exterior, with an ivory interior green or greenish-blue veins. It is semisoft to firm, crumbly, with a slightly pungent, peppery flavor. It is similar to Gorgonzola. Also known as *Moncenisio* and *Murianengo*.

Bocconcini (bow-kawn-CHEE-nee) The diminutive of *boccone*—mouthful, meaning "little mouthfuls." Bocconcini, a specialty of Campania, are very small chunks of Mozzarella cheese generally formed into little balls. They are eaten fresh after being dipped into salted water; cooked in a tomato and white wine sauce; or marinated in olive oil with many herbs and spices. *See* Mozzarella.

Bocconi Giganti (bow-kawn-CHEE-nee gee-GAHN-tee) Although the term means "giant mouthfuls," they are small balls of smoked Provolone-type cheeses. *See* Provolone.

Bra (brah) (***PDO 1996***)
- *Similar To*: Montasio and Ormea (Piedmont)
- *Region of Origin*: Bra, province of Cuneo, in Piedmont
- *History*: First produced by the Nomads
- *Type Of Milk*: Cow (small amount of goat or sheep milk can also be added)
- *Appearance And Shape*: Brown inedible exterior; white or ivory interior; wheel
- *Texture*: Firm, hard, and compact
- *Aroma And Flavor*: Sharp, spicy, salty flavor
- *Comments*: Produced in two different styles *tenero* (soft) or *duro* (hard)
- *Recommended Beverages*: Barbera, Grignolino, Nebbiolo

Branzi (BRAHN-zee) A hard, cow's milk cheese made in the region of Lombardy. It has a beige to brown inedible rind and pale yellow interior with many small holes. It is similar to *Formai de Mut dell'Alta Valle Brembana.*

Brigante (bree-GAH-teh) A sheep's milk cheese made on the island of Sardinia. It has a straw-colored exterior and pale, ivory interior with small holes. The cheese is semisoft and tangy, often used for grating with age.

Bross (brose) An extremely-strong and pungent, local cheese from Piedmont. A fresh cheese, generally Robiola, is cut up into small pieces and placed in a large bowl, where grappa and some-times white wine is poured over it. The cheese remains in contact with the grappa for at least one week, then stirred. Additional cheese and more grappa is added and this is process is repeated weekly for a total of seven weeks. Finally, the cheese is removed from the liquid, allowed to slightly dry, then eaten. Also known as *Brös, Brus*, and *Bruss.*

Brucialepre (bruh-chah-LEH-preh) A soft, cow's milk cheese shaped like a thin cake, with a creamy white interior, made in Piedmont.

Burrata (buhr-RAH-tah)
- *Region of Origin*: Apulia, Basilicata, Calabria
- *History*: Burrata was probably first made around 1920, but may have origins dating back to about 1900. Burrata, means "but-tered" in Italian.
- *Type Of Milk*: Cow and water buffalo
- *Appearance And Shape*: Glossy, white exterior; interior is pure white; Round
- *Texture*: Creamy and soft
- *Aroma And Flavor*: Mild taste and slightly tangy

- *Comments*: During the cheesemaking process, the cheese is stretched into long square strings called *lucini*. With the precision of a glass-blower, the cheesemaker blows into one *lucino*, which swells up, forming a small balloon-shaped casing into which some of the broken Mozzarella cheese pieces, along with cream and salt are added. The neck of the cheese is tied up and the Burrata is made. The cheese is generally sold in reed-like leaf wrappings and must be eaten while still fresh.
- *Recommended Beverages*: *See* Mozzarella
- *See*: Burrini

Burrini (buhr-REE-nee)

- *Also Known As*: *Burielli, Burri, Butirri, Manteca,* and occasionally *Provole*.
- *Region Of Origin*: Apulia, Basilicata, Calabria, Campania, Sicily
- *History*: It was originally used as a means to store butter before the invention of refrigeration
- *Type Of Milk*: Cow (occasionally buffalo)
- *Appearance And Shape*: Yellow interior and exterior; Small pear-shaped
- *Texture*: Soft to semisoft
- *Aroma And Flavor*: Hints of ripe fruit; flowery; sweet, buttery and slightly aromatic; mild taste and slightly tangy, similar to Provolone *dolce*.
- *Comments*: Cheeses of mild and distinctive flavor are carefully molded around a pat of sweet butter, which later will be spread on bread and eaten with the cheese. These cheeses are ripened for just a few weeks and for export are usually dipped in wax or specially packaged.
- *Recommended Beverages*: *See* Mozzarella
- *See*: Burrata

C

Caciocavallo (kah-choh-kah-VAHL-loh)
- *Similar To*: Kashkaval (Romania) and Provolone (Italy)
- *Region of Origin*: Mostly southern regions
- *History*: It is an old cheese; first mentioned in a short story by Franco Sacchetti in 1350, although some historians speculate the cheese was first mentioned abound 500 BC by Hippocrates. Supposedly, Caciocavallo got its name because two cheeses are often tied together and hung over a pole, as if astride a horse.
- *Type Of Milk*: Cow
- *Appearance And Shape*: Clay-colored or tan exterior; inedible rind; light or white interior; occasionally a few holes; the cheese is made into the shape of a pear, the upper end of which is tied-up, forming a ball
- *Texture*: Semi-hard to hard, depending on age; when hard suitable for grating
- *Aroma And Flavor*: Pungent, somewhat sharp and salty with a nutty, almond flavor and hints of anise; sometimes smoked
- *Comments*: Less than 6 months as a table cheese; suitable for grating when more than six months old. Available in three styles

dolce (sweet) with a sweet and delicate flavor; *piccante* (piquant) sharp and slightly salty; *affumicato* (smoked).
- *Recommended Beverages*: **Red**: Aglianico, Barbera, Bardolino, Cabernet Sauvignon, Grignolino, Merlot, Nebbiolo, Primitivo, Sangiovese, Valpolicella, Zinfandel: **White**: Chardonnay, Cortese, Greco di Tufo, Orvieto, Pinot Bianco, Verdicchio; **Other**: Madeira (dry); Marsala (dry); Scotch Whisky; Sherry (dry); Semisweet to Sweet Wines; Vermouth (sweet)
- *See*: Caciocavallo Silano and Ragusano

Caciocavallo Silano (kah-choh-kah-VAHL-loh see-LAH-noh) (**PDO 1996**) A semi-hard, straw-colored, cow's milk cheese made in the regions of Apulia, Basilicata, Calabria, Campania, and Molise. It is typically eaten fresh when mild and salty. As it ages, a tangy flavor develops. *See* Caciocavallo.

Caciotta (kah-CHOHT-tah)
- *Other Names*: Caciotta is produced throughout Italy under different names such as Caciotta al Tartufo, Caciotta Altopascio (Tuscany- cow and sheep milk), Caciotta di Lodi (Lombardy- cow milk), Caciotta di Siena (Tuscany- sheep milk), Caciotta d'Urbino (Marches- cow and sheep milk), Caciotta Romano (Latium- cow milk), Caciotta Norcia (Umbria- sheep milk), Caciotte del Lazio (Latium- cow and sheep milk), Caciotte delle Marche (Marches- cow milk), and Chiavara (cow, Genoa, Liguria)
- *Region of Origin*: Latium, Liguria, Lombardy, Marches, Tuscany, Umbria
- *Type Of Milk*: Made from different kinds of milk—cow, goat, sheep, or buffalo, depending on the region.
- *Appearance And Shape*: Ranges in color from white to golden yellow; Cylinders, wheels; small to medium in size
- *Texture*: Semisoft; slightly elastic

- *Aroma And Flavor*: Mild to slightly sweet and even sometimes piquant
- *Comments*: The term Caciotta means "little cheese" and is a general description of a group of cheeses made by farmers throughout Italy.
- *Recommended Beverages*: **Red:** Cabernet Sauvignon, Grignolino, Montepulciano d'Abruzzo, Petite Sirah, Pinot Noir, Sangiovese, Zinfandel; **White:** Sauvignon Blanc, Soave, Trebbiano d'Abruzzo
- *See*: Casciotta d'Urbino

Caciotta al Tartufo (kah-CHOHT-tah ahl tahr-TOO-foh) A most unusual cheese made from sheep's milk combined with trimmings of the Umbrian black truffle. *See* Caciotta.

Calcagno (kahl-KAHN-yoh) A hard, salty, and pungent sheep's milk made in Sardinia. Calcagno, used primarily for grating, often has black peppercorns in the interior. <u>Recommended Beverages</u>: Greco and Sangiovese.

Canestrato (kah-neh-STRAH-toh) A group of sheep's (also cow and goat) milk cheeses from several southern regions (Apulia, Calabria, and Sicily) that are pressed in a wicker mold (*canestro*), which leaves its imprint on the exterior of the cheese. The cheese is sometimes made from a combination of cow and sheep's milk. Also known as *Incanestrato, Pecorino Canestrato* (or *Incanestrato*), *Rigatello* and *Rigato* (which are descriptive of its ridges surface). *See* Canestrato Pugliese and Pecorino Siciliano.

Canestrato Pugliese (kah-neh-STRAH-toh puhl-YEH-zeh) (***PDO 1996***) A cylindrical-shaped, sheep's milk cheese made in the region of Apulia. It is golden-brown in color with a straw-colored interior and small holes. The cheese is rich, with a full flavor and a sweet taste. Mature versions are more aromatic. *See* Canestrato.

Cansiglio (kan-SEE-yoh) A wheel-shaped, cow's milk cheese made in Veneto. It is straw-colored with an ivory interior and small holes. It is a mild cheese with a soft, sweet taste. The cheese is sometimes smoked.

Caprini (kah-PREE-nee) A group of soft cheeses made in many regions from goat's (from *capra*, goat) milk, but nowadays mostly from cow's milk. The cheeses, which are similar to *Robiola Piemonte*, are eaten fresh with sugar or drizzled with olive oil and various herbs. It is similar to *Fagottini*. Also known as *Caprino, Caprino Piemontese*, and *Caprino Romano*. *See* Caprini di Montevecchia. <u>Recommended Beverages</u>: Frascati, Orvieto, Pinot Noir, Riesling, Pinot Grigio, Sauvignon Blanc, Soave, and Zinfandel (red).

Caprini di Montevecchia (kah-PREE-nee dee mohn-teh VEHK-kyah) A cylindrical-shaped, goat's milk cheese made in the region of Lombardy. It is generally pale white in color with a delicate aroma and pleasantly acidic flavor. *See* Caprini.

Casatella Trevigiana (kah-sah-TEHL-lah treh-vee-JAH-nah) (***PDO 2008***) A soft and creamy, round or rectangular-shaped, cow's milk cheese made in the province of Treviso, in the region of Veneto. It is rindless with an ivory-white interior, an intense aroma of milk and a sweet, slightly acidic flavor.

Casciotta d'Urbino (kah-SHOH-tah dohr-BEE-noh) (***PDO 1996***) A type of Caciotta cheese, made in the province of Pesaro and Urbino in the Marches region. It is made from a combination of sheep and cow's milk. Casciotta d'Urbino, made in ancient times, is said to be a favorite of Michelangelo and Pope Clement XIV. Supposedly the spelling of this cheese came about from a mispronunciation of Caciotta by a local servant, while others say it derived from the local dialect. *See* Caciotta.

Casiddi (kah-SEED-dee) A small, hard, goat's milk cheese made in Basilicata.

Casizolu (kah-see-ZOH-luh) A pear-shaped, cow's milk cheese made in Sardinia. It has a yellow exterior and a white to pale yellow interior, mild tasting, with a tough and elastic texture.

Castagneto (kah-stah-NYEH-toh) A fresh, disk-shaped, goat's milk cheese, wrapped in chestnut leaves, made in Piedmont.

Casteljosina (kah-stehl-YOH-see-nah) A cylindrical-shaped cow's milk cheese from Piedmont. It has an inedible crust, light gray (sometimes with red spots depending on age), with a pleasantly fragrant aroma, and a soft and rather crumbly texture.

Castelmagno (kah-stehl-MAHN-yoh) (***PDO 1996***)
- *Similar To*: Gorgonzola
- *Region Of Origin*: Castelmagno, Piedmont
- *History*: First made as early as 1277. It is named after a Roman soldier whom despite being persecuted, kept on preaching gospels and gave its name to the famous sanctuary town of Castelmagno in Grana Valley.
- *Type Of Milk*: Cow (occasionally goat and/or sheep's milk)
- *Appearance And Shape*: Blue cheese; light brown rind with white/gray spots; white-colored to pale yellow interior with no holes; Cylindrical-shaped
- *Texture*: Semisoft and creamy; crumble when aged

- *Aroma And Flavor*: Quite sharp and lightly salty; often flavored with herbs.
- *Recommended Beverages*: *See* Gorgonzola

Casu Becciu (KAH-suh BEH-chew)**, Casu Iscaldidu** (KAH-suh ees-kahl-DEE-doo)**, Casu Marzu** (KAH-suh MAHR-zoo) An unusual group of cheeses made in Sardinia from cow or goat's milk. The cheese is quite crumbly and pungently strong flavored, often referred to as "old rotter."

Cevrin di Coazze (CHEHV-reen dee koh-AHT-zeh) A round or cylindrical-shaped cheese made from a mixture of goat and cow's milk, in the province of Turin, Piedmont. The exterior is wrinkled, hard, and reddish-grey in color with yellow and white highlights depending on its age. The interior is yellowish with small holes. The texture is soft and elastic, with a strong and persistent aroma. Its flavor is salty and sharp with age.

Crescenza (kreh-SHEN-zah) A stracchino cheese made in the regions of Lombardy, Piedmont, and Veneto. Two theories emerge as to the origins of the cheese's name. The term comes from *crescere*, to grow, since the cheese tends to increase in volume if left in a warm location. Another is that Crescenza takes its name from *carzenze*, the traditional mold in which it is made. *See* Stracchino.

Crotonese (kroh-toh-NEH-seh)
- *Also Known As*: *Cotronese* and *Pecorino Crotonese*
- *Region Of Origin*: Crotone, Calabria
- *Type Of Milk*: Sheep (or sheep and goat)
- *Appearance And Shape*: Rough, orange-colored rind; white or pale straw yellow interior with small holes; cylindrical-shaped
- *Texture*: Hard and granular

- *Aroma And Flavor*: Oily, sweet, and salty; sometimes flavored with whole peppercorns
- *Comments*: A grana-type cheese
- *Recommended Beverages*: *See* Grana.
- *See*: Grana

D

Dolce Sardo (DOHL-cheh SAHR-doh) A cylindrical-shaped, cow's milk cheese from Oristano, Sardinia, which has a straw-colored exterior and ivory interior with small holes. It is soft textured, creamy, and sweet tasting.

F

Fagottini (fah-goh-TEE-nee) A fresh goat's milk cheese, pure white in color that is wrapped in parchment paper, and then tied with ratafia, is made in Piedmont. Fagottini translated means, "little bundles." It is similar to *Caprini*.

Fior di Latte (fee-OHR-eh dee LAHT-teh) A name often associated with Mozzarella cheese made from cow's milk. *See* Mozzarella.

Fiore Sardo (fee-OHR-eh SAHR-doh) (***PDO 1996***)
- *Also Known As*: Pecorino Sardo and Sardo
- *Similar To*: Pecorino Romano
- *Region Of Origin*: Sardinia
- *History*: The name Fiore Sardo means the "flower of Sardinia"
- *Type Of Milk*: Sheep (sometimes mixed with cow's milk)
- *Appearance And Shape*: Pale yellow to dark brown exterior; inedible rind; straw-yellow interior; Flat rounds
- *Texture*: Semi-hard to hard
- *Aroma And Flavor*: Mild to sharp, salty flavor depending on age

- *Comments*: Suitable for grating when hard. It is sometimes tinted with saffron.
- *Recommended Beverages*: **Red**: Aglianico, Amarone della Valpolicella, Barbera, Cabernet Sauvignon, Grenache, Grignolino, Nebbiolo, Petite Sirah, Primitivo, Sangiovese, Valpolicella, Zinfandel; **White**: Fiano di Avellino, Greco di Tufo, Sauvignon Blanc; **Other**: Marsala (dry); Semisweet to Sweet Wines; Vermouth (sweet)
- *See*: Pecorino

Foggiano (foh-JAH-noh) A cylindrical-shaped, sheep's milk (sometimes mixed with cow or goat) cheese from the city of Foggia in Apulia. It has an inedible yellow-brown exterior and straw-yellow interior. It is suitable for grating when hard.

Fontal (fohn-TAHL) A round-shaped, cow's milk cheese, made in the region of Trentino-Alto Adige. It has a waxed exterior and an ivory interior with a semi-firm, elastic texture. It is semisoft, with a taste milder than Fontina.

Fontina (fohn-TEE-nah) (***PDO 1996***)
- *Also Known As*: *Fontina d'Aosta* (Italy), *Fontinella* (Wisconsin, United States)
- *Similar To*: Bitto and Vacherin Fribourgeois
- *Region Of Origin*: Valle d'Aosta (also made in other countries including the United States)
- *History*: Possibly dating from Roman times; its origins in Lombardy date back to the eleventh century.
- *Type Of Milk*: Cow (there is a goat's milk version made in Valle d'Aosta known as *Fontini*)
- *Appearance And Shape*: Light brown exterior with an inedible rind; pale yellow interior with tiny holes; Wheel-shaped
- *Texture*: Semisoft to firm; elastic texture

- *Aroma And Flavor*: Pungent odor, reminiscent of white truffles and mushrooms; mild, sweet, nutty taste that sharpens with age
- *Comments*: It is matured in tunnels deep inside the mountains. Authentic Italian-made Fontina has a mark stenciled in purple on its outside rind. On the top will be a circle with the word "Fontina" printed across a mountain. Beware the red-waxed rind—the telltale sign of a copy.
- *Recommended Beverages*: **Red**: Barbera, Bardolino, Beaujolais, Carmenère, Dolcetto, Grignolino, Merlot, Nebbiolo, Pinot Noir, Sangiovese, Valpolicella, Zinfandel; **White**: Chardonnay, Cortese, Friulano, Gewürztraminer, Orvieto, Pinot Bianco, Pinot Grigio, Riesling, Sauvignon Blanc, Soave, Verdicchio, Zinfandel; **Other**: Champagne and Sparkling Wine (dry); Madeira (dry); Marsala (dry); Sherry (dry)
- *See*: Fontal

Formaggella del Luinese (fohr-mah-JEHL-ah loo-eh-NEH-zeh) (**PDO 2011**) A soft goat's milk cheese made in the region of Lombardy. It has a thin crust, subject to mold and a cream-colored interior, which is soft. The flavor becomes quite strong with age. *See* Formaggelle.

Formaggelle (fohr-mah-JEHL-leh) A group of soft cheeses made from cow, goat, or sheep's milk in the mountainous area of Northern Italy. These cheeses are eaten fresh, seasoned with salt, pepper, olive oil, and various herbs or salted and aged. Some examples are *Formaggella Bernarda, Formaggella del Luinese, Formaggella della Val Bavona*, and *Formaggella Ticinese*.

Formaggio di Fossa di Sogliano (fohr-MAHJ-joh dee FOH-sah dee sohl-YAH-noh) (**PDO 2009**) A cheese made from either sheep's milk, cow's milk, or a mixture of the two, in the regions of Emilia-Romagna and Marches. During the months of April or May, bundles of cheese are kept tightly packed, then put into a *fossa*, a (ten to 15 foot deep) pit dug into the ground and lined with straw. The pit is prepared by burning straw inside to remove moisture and sterilize the space. The cheese is tightly wrapped and the pit is sealed with sand and stone to prevent oxidation. The cheese ages until its traditional unpacking day St. Catherine's Day (November 25). The resultant cheese is deep amber in color with a highly pungent odor, and creamy center. This technique dates back to the fifteenth century.

Formai de Mut dell'Alta Valle Brembana (fohr-MIE deh moot dehl-AHL-tah VAHL-leh brehm-BAH-nah) (***PDO 1996***) A cow's milk cheese made in the Valle Brembana, in the region of Lombardy. The word *mut* literally means "mountain" in the local dialect, and in this instance refers to the Alps. It is similar to *Branzi* and *Fontina*.

Fresa (FREH-zah) A yellow-colored, soft, mild, sweet tasting cheese made from cow or goat's milk in Sardinia.

G

Giuncata (joon-KAH-tah) A fresh, soft, cow's (also sheep and goat) milk cheese; a local delicacy of many regions. This cheese, which gets its name from the *giunchi* in which it's wrapped, takes on the shape of the wrappings.

Gorgonzola (gohr-gohn-ZOH-lah) (***PDO 1996***)
- *Also Known As*: *Stracchino di Gorgonzola*
- *Similar To*: *Bolina* (Denmark), and many other blue-cheeses
- *Region Of Origin*: Lombardy and Piedmont (also made in the United States)
- *History*: First made in 879 AD in the city of Gorgonzola near Milan, but now little is made there. Originally the cheese was called *Stracchino di Gorgonzola*, supposedly derived from the word *stracco* or weary, which was what the cows were said to be after their annual trek down from the summer pastures in the Alps.
- *Type Of Milk*: Cow
- *Appearance And Shape*: Reddish-brown inedible rind; pale yellow interior with greenish-blue veins; Cylindrical and flat

loaves; *Penicillium glaucum* is added to the cheese to obtain its green-blue veining.

- *Texture*: Creamy and semisoft to firm; pasty; sometimes crumbly
- *Aroma And Flavor*: Tangy, superbly rich, slightly pungent, salty, spicy-peppery flavor
- *Comments*: The blue veins are produced by pricking the cheese with long copper, steel, or brass needles, which expose the cheese to the air in different points, helping to form the mold. Gorgonzola is made in two styles the *dolce* or *burroso* (sweet or buttery) and the *piccante* (piquant). *Dolce* Gorgonzola has a sweet, nutty flavor and creamy texture. *Piccante* Gorgonzola is sharper in flavor and slightly firmer.
- *Recommended Beverages*: **Red**: Aglianico, Amarone della Valpolicella, Barbera, Cabernet Sauvignon, Dolcetto, Grignolino, Montefalco Sagrantino, Nebbiolo, Primitivo, Sangiovese, Valpolicella, Zinfandel; **White:** Friulano, Gewürztraminer, Sauvignon Blanc; **Other**: Brandy (grapes); Brandy (fruit); Champagne and Sparkling Wine (semisweet to sweet); Grappa; Madeira (dry); Marsala (dry); Port; Sherry (dry); Vin Santo; Semisweet to Sweet Wines; Vermouth (sweet)
- *See*: Gorgonzola Bianco

Gorgonzola Bianco (gohr-gohn-ZOH-lah bee-AHN-koh) A rarely produced, un-veined Gorgonzola cheese. Also known as *Pannarone* and *Pannerone*. *See* Gorgonzola.

Grana (GRAH-nah) A generic name for a group of hard cow, sheep, or even goat's milk cheeses, made throughout Italy (also other countries), which have a flaky, grainy or *granular* texture. These cheeses are suitable for grating when they begin to get old. Some examples are *Asiago, Bagozzo, Crotonese, Grana Padano, Granone Lodigiano, Kefalotyri, Parmigiano-Reggiano, Pecorino, Piave,*

Sapsago, *Sbrinz*, and *Vacchino Romano*. Therefore, "all Parmigiano-Reggiano cheeses are *grana*, but not all *grana* are Parmigiano-Reggiano." Italian hard cheeses were once referred to as *cacio duro*. The word "Grana" is legally protected by Grana Padano Protected Designation of Origin, such that only Grana Padano can use the term to sell its produce in EU countries. <u>Recommended Beverages</u>: **Red** Aglianico, Amarone della Valpolicella, Barbera, Bardolino, Cabernet Sauvignon, Dolcetto, Grignolino, Lambrusco, Merlot, Montepulciano d'Abruzzo, Nebbiolo, Petite Sirah, Pinot Noir, Primitivo, Sangiovese, Valpolicella, Zinfandel: **White**: Chardonnay, Cortese, Fiano di Avellino, Friulano, Gewürztraminer, Orvieto, Pinot Grigio, Riesling, Sauvignon Blanc, Trebbiano d'Abruzzo, Verdicchio; **Other**: Marsala (dry); Port; Champagne and Sparkling Wine (dry); Sherry (dry); Semisweet to Sweet Wines; Vermouth (sweet); Bourbon and Tennessee Whiskey

Grana Padano (GRAH-nah pah-DAH-noh) (*PDO 1996*)
- *Similar To*: Parmigiano-Reggiano
- *Region of Origin*: Northern Italy (Emilia-Romagna, Lombardy, Piedmont, Trentino-Alto Adige, Veneto)
- *Type Of Milk*: Cow
- *Appearance And Shape*: White to yellow exterior with an oily sheen; white or pale yellow interior with tiny holes; Drum-shaped
- *Texture*: Hard and flaky, granular texture
- *Aroma And Flavor*: Fragrant aroma and delicate tasting
- *Comments*: Suitable for grating when hard. The consortium seal "Grana Padano" is repeatedly stamped around the rind as a guarantee of authenticity and quality. Its origins date back to the eleventh century. The name Padano means "of the Po," a river that traverses through Piedmont and Lombardy.
- *Recommended Beverages*: *See* Grana
- *See*: Grana

Granone Lodigiano (grah-NOH-neh loh-dee-JAHN-oh) A *grana*-type cheese from the town of Lodi in southern Lombardy. *See* Grana.

Grasso d'Alpe (GRAH-soh DAHL-peh) A soft textured cow's milk cheese with a pale yellow exterior, dotted with holes; made in the region of Piedmont.

Gravina (grah-VEE-nah) A semi-hard, ball-shaped, cow's milk cheese produced in Basilicata and Apulia.

I

Italico (ee-TAH-lee-coh) A group of semisoft, delicately-flavored cheeses (Bel Paese and Robiola Piemonte are examples) made in Lombardy, which according to a Ministerial Decree, issued by Mussolini on May 10, 1941, required these cheeses to use the name Italico. The intention was to standardize the many commercial definitions of all the cheeses with similar qualities to be found in the territory. Now Italico is a recognized cheese in its own right.

M

Mascarpone (mahs-kahr-POH-neh)
- _Also Known As_: Also spelled _Mascherpone_
- _Similar To_: Cream Cheese
- _Region Of Origin_: Lombardy (also made in other countries including the United States)
- _History_: The cheese dates back at least to the sixteenth, although some say as early as the twelfth century.
- _Type Of Milk_: Cow. There is a rare, water buffalo-milk (Mascarpone di bufala) version produced in the region of Campania.
- _Appearance And Shape_: White exterior and interior; Ball-shaped; often sold in muslin bags or small tubs
- _Texture_: Soft and smooth; triple-crème cheese
- _Aroma And Flavor_: Delicate, buttery flavor; tastes like whipped cream cheese
- _Comments_: Often has candied fruit in the center; good dessert cheese, often flavored with cinnamon, coffee, powdered chocolate, sugar, or rum and liqueurs.
- _Recommended Beverages_: _See_ Ricotta

Montasio (mohn-TAH-see-oh) (*PDO 1996*)
- *Similar To*: Asiago, Bitto, and Bra
- *Region Of Origin*: Friuli-Venezia Giulia and Veneto
- *History*: First produced in the thirteenth century in the convent of Moggio
- *Type Of Milk*: Cow
- *Appearance And Shape*: Straw-colored exterior with inedible rind; light yellow interior with irregular holes; Wheel-shaped
- *Texture*: Semisoft to hard
- *Aroma And Flavor*: Salty and piquant, and sometimes nutty
- *Comments*: Suitable for grating when hard. Three varieties are made– *fresco* (fresh); *semistagionato* (partially aged), and *vecchio* (well aged). Montasio cheese will have a large letter "M" on its outer wrapper.
- *Recommended Beverages*: Dolcetto, Pinot Grigio, and Sauvignon Blanc.

Monte Veronese (MOHN-teh vehr-oh-NEH-zeh) (*PDO 1996*) A semi-firm, cow's milk cheese made in the region of Veneto, since the thirteenth century. It has a straw-colored exterior and a white interior with tiny holes. It has an elastic texture and a mild sharpness on the finish. The cheese comes in three versions, Monte Veronese *Latte intero* (fresh); Monte Veronese *d'Allevo* (aged more than 60 days); and Monte Veronese *d'Allevo Vecchio* (mature: aged for about one year).

Montebore (mohn-teh-BOHR-eh) A cone-shaped cheese made from cow's and sheep's milk in the region of Piedmont. It has a white or pale yellow exterior and straw-colored interior with tiny holes; semisoft to hard (depending on age), with a tangy flavor that becomes quite pungent with age. It is suitable for grating when hard.

Morlacco (mohr-LAHK-koh) A cylindrical-shaped, cow's milk cheese, made in the region of Veneto. Named after the *Morlacca* nomadic people who arrived in Italy as shepherds from the Balkans. Its exterior bears the imprint from the basket mold. It has an ivory interior with small, irregular holes. It is semi-hard in texture with a delicate floral fruity aroma.

Moro del Logudoro (MOH-roh dehl loh-goo-DOH-roh) A semisoft, wheel-shaped, sheep's milk cheese, made in Sardinia, which has a soft and creamy texture, and is often eaten for dessert. After several months of aging, it become hard and is suitable for grating.

Mozzarella (mohtz-ah-REHL-lah)
- *Similar To*: Mano (Venezuela)
- *Region Of Origin*: Campania (also made in the United States)
- *History*: It dates back to the 1400s in southern Italy.
- *Type Of Milk*: Water buffalo milk in Italy (cow's milk most other countries). The buffaloes are bred in Campania and their low-yield milk is utilized. The white buffaloes are descendants of the Indian water buffalo brought to Campania in the sixteenth century.
- *Appearance And Shape*: Creamy white exterior and interior; rindless; Various shapes and sizes including round, rectangular, and salami-shaped; When twisted or braided it's called *treccia*.
- *Texture*: Soft, moist, and quite pliable, sometimes almost elastic
- *Aroma And Flavor*: Mild, delicate, slightly tart-sour flavor
- *Comments*: The name "mozzarella" is derived from the word *mozzare*, which means "to top off or cut," referring to the hand method of production. When freshly made, it drips profusely with whey. A smoked version, called *mozzarella affumicata*, is also produced.

- _Recommended Beverages_: **Red**: Bardolino, Beaujolais, Cabernet Sauvignon, Dolcetto, Nebbiolo, Sangiovese, Valpolicella, Zinfandel; **White**: Chardonnay, Chenin Blanc, Frascati, Gewürztraminer, Orvieto, Pinot Bianco, Pinot Grigio, Riesling, Sauvignon Blanc, Soave, Verdicchio, Zinfandel; **Other**: Marsala (dry); Rosé (dry); Sherry (dry); Semisweet to Sweet Wines; Vermouth (sweet)
- _See_: Bocconcini, Fior di Latte, Mozzarella di Bufala Campana, and Scamorza

Mozzarella di Bufala Campana (mohtz-ah-REHL-lah dee BOO-fah-lah kahm-PAH-nah) (**_PDO_ 1996**) A cheese made from _water buffalo_, produced in the regions of Apulia, Campania, Latium, and Molise. The cheese is delicate and milky with a soft texture and slight gamey flavor. _See_ Mozzarella.

Murazzano (moo-rahtz-ZAHN-noh) (**_PDO_ 1996**) A soft and semisoft, disk-shaped, sheep's (or cow) milk cheese made in Piedmont. It has a pure white, rindless exterior and a milky white to pale yellow interior, and elastic texture. _See_ Robiola Piemonte.

N

Nostrano Valtrompia (noh-STRAH-noh vahl-TROHM-pyah) (***PDO* 2012**) A hard, wheel-shaped, cow's milk cheese made in the region of Lombardy. It has a yellow-orange exterior and pale yellow interior often colored with saffron.

P

Paglia (PAHL-yah) A disk-shaped cheese made from cow, sheep, or goat's milk (or any combination) in Lombardy and Piedmont. It is white or pale yellow in color with a pleasing aromatic scent of garlic, mushrooms, and wild onions. It is soft and creamy, with a strong, almost sour-taste. The word *paglia* translates to mean "straw," because the cheese is aged on straw, and often wrapped in paper. Pagliarini is often eaten drizzled with olive oil and salt and pepper. It is similar to *Brie, Camembert,* and *Toma.* Also known as *Pagliarini.*

Parmigiano-Reggiano (pahr-mee-JAH-noh rehj-JAHN-oh) (**PDO 1996**)
- *Also Known As*: *Parmesan* and *Parmigiano*
- *Similar To*: Asiago (aged), Bagozzo (Italy), Grana Padano (Italy), Kefalotyri (Greece), Mahón (Spain), Manchego (Spain), Monterey Jack (aged), and Paški Sir (Croatia)
- *Region Of Origin*: Provinces of Parma, Reggio Emilia, and Modena, in Emilia-Romagna
- *History*: First made in the eleventh or twelfth century

- *Type Of Milk*: Cow; the whey from the milk is fed to the pigs used for Prosciutto di Parma.
- *Appearance And Shape*: Light, moist looking, straw-yellow exterior; inedible golden yellow rind with an oily sheen; straw-yellow interior comprised of tiny, pale-gold crystals; Wheels
- *Texture*: Hard, granular, and flaky depending on age; the crystal-like texture is due to protein crystals that form when amino acids break down during the aging process. The longer the cheese ages, the more "crunch" to enjoy.
- *Aroma And Flavor*: Complex, mellow flavor, slightly nutty, buttery, and salty in taste; granular smoothness and intensely flavorful. Other cheeses get sharper as they age; Parmigiano-Reggiano becomes mellower.
- *Comments*: Can be eaten in bite-size chunks when young; when old, suitable for grating when hard. When buying the cheese examine it carefully. It should be a uniform moist but pale amber color and should be without any telltale signs of dryness, white patches or a white rim next to the rind. The rind that encases the cheese is imprinted with a repeating pattern with the stippled words "Parmigiano-Reggiano," the official title bestowed by governmental decree in 1939. In 1934, the consorzio was established to regulate the production and control quality. Then in 1995, Italian law designated the provinces of Parma, Reggio Emilia, and Modena in their entirety and portions of the provinces of Bologna and Mantua as controlled cheese-making districts. In addition to the stippled words, the wheel is branded with the *Consorzio Tutela Parmigiano-Reggiano* oval, which is a quality assurance that the cheese has been produced at government certified dairies in the Parma and Reggio provinces of Emilia-Romagna. Cheeses simply labeled "Parmigiano" do not come from Italy and are lower in quality. Grating cheese from other areas is labeled "grana" and varies in quality. The minimum aging time is 12 months (the highest of all cheeses). There

are three reference aging: over 18 months, over 22 months, over 30 months. Parmigiano-Reggiano is a grana-type cheese.

- *Recommended Beverages*: **Red**: Aglianico, Amarone della Valpolicella, Barbera, Bardolino, Cabernet Sauvignon, Dolcetto, Grignolino, Lambrusco, Merlot, Montepulciano d'Abruzzo, Nebbiolo, Petite Sirah, Pinot Noir, Primitivo, Sangiovese, Valpolicella, Zinfandel: **White**: Chardonnay, Cortese, Fiano di Avellino, Friulano, Gewürztraminer, Orvieto, Pinot Grigio, Riesling, Sauvignon Blanc, Trebbiano d'Abruzzo, Verdicchio; **Other**: Madeira (dry); Marsala (dry); Port; Champagne and Sparkling Wine (dry); Sherry (dry); Semisweet to Sweet Wines; Vermouth (sweet); Vin Santo; Bourbon and Tennessee Whiskey
- *See*: Grana

Pastorella del Cerreto di Sorano (pahs-tohr-REHL-lah dehl cheh-REHT-toh dee sohr-AH-noh) A wheel-shaped, cheese made from sheep and cow's milk in the region of Tuscany. Its exterior is red-brick in color (rubbed with the pulp of tomatoes) with a buttery texture, and soft and creamy interior with a sweet pleasant taste. *See* Bel Paese.

Pecorino (peh-koh-REE-noh) A generic term for a group of cheeses produced throughout Italy, entirely from sheep's (*pecora*) milk. The cheese comes in many versions; soft or hard, fresh or aged, mild or piquant. There are substantial differences, furthermore, among pecorino cheeses from different regions. *See* Canestrato, Fiore Sardo, Foggiano, Grana, Pecorino di Filiano, Pecorino di San Leo, Pecorino Romano, Pecorino Senese, Pecorino Siciliano, and Pecorino Toscano.
Recommended Beverages: **Red**: Aglianico, Amarone della Valpolicella, Barbera, Bardolino, Cabernet Sauvignon, Dolcetto, Grignolino, Lambrusco, Merlot, Montefalco Sagrantino,

Montepulciano d'Abruzzo, Nebbiolo, Petite Sirah, Pinot Noir, Primitivo, Sangiovese, Valpolicella, Zinfandel: **White**: Catarratto, Chardonnay, Cortese, Fiano di Avellino, Friulano, Gewürztraminer, Orvieto, Pinot Grigio, Riesling, Sauvignon Blanc, Trebbiano d'Abruzzo, Verdicchio; **Other**: Champagne and Sparkling Wine (dry); Madeira (dry); Marsala (dry); Port; Sherry (dry); Semisweet to Sweet Wines; Vermouth (sweet); Vin Santo; Bourbon and Tennessee Whiskey

Pecorino Crotonese (peh-koh-REE-noh kroh-toh-NEH-seh) (*PDO* **2014**) A wheel-shaped, sheep's milk cheese made in the region of Calabria. The exterior is orange-reddish in color with markings from the basket it which it was aged. It has a straw-yellow interior with no holes, a semi-hard texture and slightly salty taste.

Pecorino delle Balze Volterrane (peh-koh-REE-noh DEHL-leh BAHL-zeh vohl-tehr-RAH-neh) (*PDO* **2015**) A wheel-shaped, sheep's milk cheese made in the region of Tuscany. It has an inedible yellow-brown rind (often rubbed with ashes) and pale yellow interior with many holes. It has a semi-hard texture and intense flavor.

Pecorino di Filiano (peh-koh-REE-noh dee fee-YAH-noh) (*PDO* **2007**) A semi-firm, sheep's milk cheese named for a for a village in the Potenza province of Basilicata. It is cylindrical in shape with a golden yellow to dark brown exterior and yellow interior. Its exterior is often rubbed with extra virgin olive oil and wine vinegar. Its flavor is tart and salty, with hints of tasted hazelnuts. *See* Pecorino.

Pecorino di Picinisco (peh-koh-REE-noh dee pee-chee-NEE-skoh) (*PDO* **2013**) A wheel-shaped, sheep's milk cheese made in the region of Latium. It has a straw-yellow exterior with markings from the basket it which it was aged and a pale yellow interior with small holes. It has a firm texture and a nutty, slightly salty taste.

Pecorino di San Leo (peh-koh-REE-noh dee sahn LEH-oh) A sheep's milk cheese from the town of San Leo in the region of Marches. This soft cheese, resembling *ricotta*, is often wrapped in walnut leaves and kept in earthenware jars until it is well aged. *See* Pecorino.

Pecorino Romano (peh-koh-REE-noh roh-MAH-noh) (**PDO 1996**)
- *Similar To*: Fiore Sardo
- *Region Of Origin*: Latium, Sardinia, and Tuscany
- *History*: Probably the most ancient cheese produced in Italy, which has been traced back to the first century A.D.
- *Type Of Milk*: Sheep
- *Appearance And Shape*: Hard, brittle, dark brown to black-colored (often with lampblack), inedible rind; white or straw-colored exterior and interior; Wheels; embossed on the rind with a sheep's head and the words "*Pecorino Romano*," which ensures authenticity.
- *Texture*: Hard and granular, which becomes flaky with age
- *Aroma And Flavor*: Complex aroma, sharp, slightly salty flavor. With age, it becomes saltier.
- *Comments*: A *grana-type* cheese. Authentic Pecorino Romano will have on its outer rind a rhombus (diamond) inside which appears the stylized head of a sheep with the inscription "*Pecorino Romano*." Under it, the month and year of production of the form, the number of the province and the serial number of the producer. Suitable for grating when hard.
- *Recommended Beverages*: *See* Pecorino
- *See*: Grana and Pecorino

Pecorino Senese (peh-koh-REE-noh seh-NEH-zeh) A cylindrical-shaped, sheep's milk cheese from Tuscany. Its rind is reddish brown in color (rubbed with olive oil and tomato paste; sometimes wood ashes), with a light-yellow interior with tiny holes. It is semi-hard, with a slightly sharp and delicate flavor. *See* Pecorino

Pecorino Siciliano (peh-koh-REE-noh see-cheel-ee-YAH-noh) (***PDO 1996***)
- *Region Of Origin*: Sicily
- *Type Of Milk*: Sheep
- *Appearance And Shape*: Light yellow exterior with the imprint of the basket in which it was pressed; inedible rind; white or straw-colored interior with few holes; Cylindrical blocks
- *Texture*: Hard and granular, which becomes flaky with age
- *Aroma And Flavor*: Complex aroma, sharp, slightly salty flavor. With age, it becomes saltier.
- *Comments*: The Pecorino cheeses of Sicily are collectively known as Pecorino Siciliano. There are two other varieties *Canestrato* or *Incanestrato* (formed in straw baskets) and another called *Pepato*, seasoned with whole black peppercorns. Suitable for grating when hard.
- *Recommended Beverages*: *See* Pecorino
- *See*: Canestrato, Grana, and Pecorino

Pecorino Toscano (peh-koh-REE-noh tohs-KAH-noh) (***PDO 1996***) A wheel-shaped, sheep's milk cheese made in Tuscany. It has a pale yellow exterior and beige to yellow, flaky interior. The cheese is semi-hard to hard, depending on aging and is suitable for grating when aged. Documents prior to the late 1400s, refer to Pecorino Toscano as *marzolino* cheese, referring to the month of March (*marzo* in Italian), when production began. *See* Grana and Pecorino.

Piacentinu Ennese (pee-ah-CHEN-tee-noo eh-NEH-zeh) (**PDO 2011**) A hard, sheep's milk cheese made in the province of Enna in Sicily. The name of the cheese implies that it is produced in the city of Piacenza in Lombardy. The cheese is wheel-shaped, with marked incisions caused by the basket into which the cheese ages and the deep yellow-orange exterior is due to the use of saffron. The interior is bright yellow, speckled with black peppercorns. The cheese has been made since the 1100s. The cheese is sometimes referred to as *Grana Piacentino* or *Piacentino*.

Piave (PYAH-veh) (**PDO 2010**) A cow's milk cheese that is named after the Piave River, in the region of Veneto. It is a hard cheese, straw-colored, with a dense, flaky texture without any holes. It has a slight almond bitterness and when aged, it is suitable for grating. *See* Grana.

Prescinseua (pre-sheen-seh-WAH) A fresh and spreadable cow's milk cheese, sort of halfway between ricotta and Greek yogurt, made in the region of Liguria.

Pressato (preh-SAHT-toh) A semi-hard to hard, wheel-shaped, cow's milk cheese made in Veneto. It has a light yellow inedible exterior and a straw-yellow interior with irregular holes. It has a mild and slightly sweet flavor and is suitable for grating when hard. *See* Asiago. <u>Recommended Beverages</u>: Cabernet Sauvignon, Champagne and Sparkling Wine (dry).

Primo Sale (PREE-moh SAH-leh) (**PDO 1996**) A round-shaped, sheep's milk cheese made in the region of Sicily. It has a white rindless exterior with markings from the basket in which it was aged. The interior is white with holes and is sometimes flavored with red or black peppercorns. Semisoft texture and mild, slightly salty taste. The name itself literally means "first salt" and is used to describe early stages of maturation.

Provola (PROH-voh-lah) A small version of provolone, which may be smoked or unsmoked.

Provolone (proh-voh-LOH-neh)
- _Similar To_: Caciocavallo and Golan (Israel- sheep milk)
- _Region Of Origin_: Southern, Italy (also made in the United States)
- _History_: The name Provolone comes from a local, round cheese (made in Naples), which used to be called _Provva_.
- _Type Of Milk_: Cow (once made from water buffalo milk)
- _Appearance And Shape_: Light golden yellow color, waxed exterior; creamy ivory interior; various shapes and sizes including rectangular, ball, oval, round, wheels, and giant salami (known as _gigante_)
- _Texture_: Smooth; firm to hard
- _Aroma And Flavor_: Mild to quite tangy and even sharp, depending on the age of the cheese
- _Comments_: Suitable for grating when hard; sometimes smoked. Available in three styles _dolce_ (sweet) with a sweet and delicate flavor, which is aged for two to three months; _piccante_ (piquant) sharp and slightly salty, which is aged slightly longer; _affumicato_ (smoked) for about one week then aged for about two months. When well aged, Provolone is also suitable for grating.
- _Recommended Beverages_: **Red** Aglianico, Amarone della Valpolicella, Barbera, Bardolino, Cabernet Sauvignon, Dolcetto, Grignolino, Merlot, Nebbiolo, Petite Sirah, Pinot Noir, Primitivo, Sangiovese, Valpolicella, Zinfandel; **White**: Chardonnay, Friulano, Gewürztraminer, Greco di Tufo, Orvieto, Riesling, Sauvignon Blanc, Soave; **Other**: Madeira (dry); Marsala (dry);

Sherry (dry); Semisweet to Sweet Wines; Vermouth (sweet); Vin Santo
- *See*: Bocconi Giganti, Provola, Provolone del Monaco, and Provolone Valpadana.

Provolone del Monaco (proh-voh-LOH-neh dehl MOH-ah-koh) (**PDO 2010**) A semi-hard, cow's milk cheese from the region of Campania, which has a russet exterior and hazelnut color interior. It is cylinder-shaped with a pleasing sweet buttery flavor and a light, pleasant taste. *See* Provolone.

Provolone Lombardo (proh-voh-LOH-neh lom-BAHR-doh) A Provolone cheese made in Lombardy's provinces of Brescia and Cremona. *See* Provolone.

Provolone Valpadana (proh-voh-LOH-neh vahl-pah-DAH-nah) (**PDO 1996**) A cow's milk cheese, aged several months, which is made in the regions of Emilia-Romagna, Lombardy, Trentino-Aldo Adige, and Veneto. It has a firm texture and relatively mild aroma, which sharpens with age. *See* Provolone.

Puzzone di Moena (pootz-ZOH-neh dee moh-EH-nah) (*Italy*) (**PDO 2014**) A wheel-shaped, cow's milk cheese made in the region of Trentino-Alto Adige. It has a thin orange rind under a layer of wax. Interior is light straw-yellow colored with medium-sized holes. It has an elastic, semi-hard texture and an intense, very strong aroma of dried leaves and moss.

Q

Quartirolo Lombardo (qwahr-tee-ROH-loh lom-BAHR-doh) (**PDO 1996**)

- _Similar To_: Taleggio
- _Region Of Origin_: Lombardy
- _History_: It is said that the cheese was being produced before the year 1,000 in Val Taleggio, in the Lombard pre-Alps.
- _Type Of Milk_: Cow
- _Appearance And Shape_: The thin and soft exterior is pinkish-white when young, turning a reddish gray-green with age; interior chalky white to pale yellow, darkens with age; Square or rectangular-shaped
- _Texture_: Soft and lumpy
- _Aroma And Flavor_: Slightly sour and acidic in the fresh cheese; light mushroom flavor intensifies with age.
- _Comments_: This cheese is given this name because the milk used comes from cows fed with the fourth cutting of the grass (_quartirola grass_).
- _Recommended Beverages_: _See_ Taleggio

R

Ragusano (rah-goo-ZAH-noh) (***PDO 1996***) A cube-shaped, cow's milk cheese made in Ragusa, Sicily. It is one of the oldest cheeses in Sicily with evidence dating as early as 1500. The exterior is smooth, thin and exhibits a yellowish-golden color that deepens as the cheese ages. It is semi-hard, with a white to straw-yellow interior and few holes. The cheese is sometimes smoked. Ragusano was formerly known as *Caciocavallo Ragusano. See* Caciocavallo.

Raschera (RAHS-kehr-ah) (***PDO 1996***) A round or square-shaped cheese, made from cow's milk (sometimes mixed with goat or sheep's milk), made in Piedmont. It has a semi-hard, yellow exterior and an ivory interior with irregular holes. The taste is buttery, slightly salty, and richly flavored; moderately sharp with age. Also known as *Raschiera*.

Raviggiolo (rah-vee-JOH-loh) A soft and creamy, cow's (sometimes goat or sheep's milk added) cheese, made in many regions.

It is similar in style to *Ricotta* and often sold in plastic wicker baskets.

Ricotta (ree-KOHT-tah)
- *Also Known As*: *Brocotte* and *Céracée* (France)
- *Similar To*: Cacio Ricotta (Italy- sheep milk), Lor Peyniri (Turkey), Manouri (Greece- sheep milk), Mató (Spain), Raviggiolo (Italy), Requeijão (Brazil), Requeijão (Portugal-sheep milk), Requesón (Portugal- sheep milk), and Sérac (Switzerland)
- *Region Of Origin*: Italy (also made in the United States and some European countries)
- *History*: The production of ricotta in Italy is old, dating back to the Bronze Age.
- *Type Of Milk*: Cow (sometimes sheep, goat, water buffalo)
- *Appearance And Shape*: Pure white color; Tubs or containers
- *Texture*: Soft, moist body
- *Aroma And Flavor*: Mild, semisweet flavor, slightly salty
- *Comments*: The word *ricotta* means "recooked" as the cheese is a by-product of cheesemaking; it is made from the coagulated substance in whey. There are several types of Ricotta—*Ricotta Moliterna*, *Ricotta Piemontese*, and *Ricotta Romana*.
- *Recommended Beverages*: **Red**: Barbera, Bardolino, Dolcetto; **White**: Chardonnay, Chenin Blanc, Frascati, Gewürztraminer, Orvieto, Pinot Bianco, Pinot Grigio, Riesling, Sauvignon Blanc, Soave, Verdicchio; **Other**: Champagne and Sparkling Wine (semisweet to sweet); Rosé (dry)
- *See*: Ricotta di Bufala Campana and Ricotta Salata

Ricotta di Bufala Campana (ree-KOHT-tah dee BOO-fah-lah kahm-PAH-nah) (**PDO 2010**) A water buffalo's milk cheese made in the regions of Apulia, Campania, Latium, and Molise.

The cheese is made from the whey, which remains after the production of Mozzarella di Bufala Campana. It has a pure white rindless exterior with markings from the plastic tub it was made in. It is very soft and mild tasting. *See* Ricotta.

Ricotta Moliterna (ree-KOHT-tah moh-lee-TEHR-nah) A truncated-shaped, sheep's milk ricotta cheese made in Sardinia. It is white in color; semisoft and slightly salty. *See* Ricotta.

Ricotta Piemontese (ree-KOHT-tah pyeh-mohn-TEH-zeh) A cow's milk Ricotta cheese to which 10 percent whole milk is added. It is smoother and slightly blander than Ricotta. *See* Ricotta.

Ricotta Romana (ree-KOHT-tah roh-MAHN-ah) (***PDO 2005***) A sheep's milk ricotta cheese made in the region of Latium. It is packed in truncated conical wicker, plastic, or metal baskets. *See* Ricotta.

Ricotta Salata (ree-KOHT-tah sah-LAH-tah) A salted and pressed, wheel-shaped, sheep's milk cheese made in many regions including Apulia, Campania, Latium, and Sicily. It has a pure white exterior and interior and can be eaten young as a sliceable cheese; when mature used for grating. It is similar to *Baccellone* and *Ricotta Siciliana*.

Robiola delle Langhe (roh-bee-OH-lah DEHL-leh LAHN-geh) A cheese made from cow's and sheep's milk in Piedmont *See* Robiola Piemonte.

Robiola di Bossolasco (roh-bee-OH-lah dee bohs-soh-LA-HS-koh) A cylindrical-shaped, cheese made from cow and sheep's milk in Piedmont. It has a straw-yellow rind and a soft, white grainy interior with small holes. Also known as *Tuma de Bossolasco*. *See* Robiola Piemonte.

Robiola di Cocconato (roh-bee-OH-lah dee koh-koh-NAH-toh) A cylindrical-shaped cheese made from cow's milk in Piedmont. It is rindless with a white exterior; soft, creamy, ivory interior and tangy flavor. *See* Robiola Piemonte.

Robiola di Roccaverano (roh-bee-OH-lah dee ROH-kah-vehr-AH-noh) (**PDO 1996**) A flat, cylindrical-shaped cheese made from cow, goat, or sheep's milk in the provinces of Asti and Alessandria, in the region of Piedmont. This rindless cheese is wrapped in chestnut leaves and has slightly straw-yellow color. With age, the cheese develops a reddish, sticky exterior. A white interior with a fresh, yet pleasantly sour, spicy, and mild flavor. *See* Robiola Piemonte.

Robiola Piemonte (roh-bee-OH-lah pyeh-MOHN-teh) A group of fresh cheeses made in Piedmont, from cow, goat, sheep, or a combination of the milks. Robiola is made into either cylinders or flat bars. Robiola cheeses have a white or pale yellow rindless exterior and a soft, creamy texture, with spicy, piquant, salty flavors. Some varieties include *Robiola d'Alba, Robiola delle Langhe, Robiola di Bossolasco, Robiola di Cocconato,* and *Robiola di Roccaverano. See* Caprini and Murazzano. <u>Recommended Beverages</u>: Bardolino, Cortese, Dolcetto, Grignolino, Merlot, Nebbiolo, Orvieto, Pinot Grigio, Riesling, Sangiovese, Sauvignon Blanc, and Soave.

Romano: The name adopted in the United States for hard, cow, goat, or sheep's milk cheese, which have some similarity to *Pecorino* cheeses.

S

Salva Cremasco (SAHL-vah kreh-MAH-skoh) (***PDO 2012***) A square-shaped, cow's milk cheese made in the region of Lombardy. The dark, grey-brown inedible rind is washed with olive oil to keep it pliable, yet firm. It has a yellow interior with small holes, and a fresh, yet sharp taste.

Scamorza (skah-MOHR-tzah)
- _Similar To_: Mozzarella
- _Region Of Origin_: Abruzzo, Apulia, Calabria, Campania, Molise
- _Type Of Milk_: Cow; originally made with buffalo milk
- _Appearance And Shape_: Light yellow, rindless exterior; Pear-shaped or oval
- _Texture_: Soft to semisoft
- _Aroma And Flavor_: Mild and slightly salty taste
- _Comments_: Sometimes slightly smoked (*affumicato*), which gives an earthy, somewhat mushroom flavor. In southern dialect, the name *scamorza* means "dunce."
- _Recommended Beverages_: **Red**: Bardolino, Beaujolais, Cabernet Sauvignon, Dolcetto, Nebbiolo, Sangiovese, Valpolicella,

Zinfandel; **White**: Chardonnay, Chenin Blanc, Frascati, Gewürztraminer, Orvieto, Pinot Bianco, Pinot Grigio, Riesling, Sauvignon Blanc, Soave, Verdicchio, Zinfandel; **Other**: Madeira (dry); Marsala (dry); Rosé (dry); Sherry (dry); Semisweet to Sweet Wines; Vermouth (sweet)

Scanno (SKAHN-noh) A sheep's milk cheese from the mountain village of Scanno in Abruzzo, traditionally eaten with fresh fruit. The exterior is black with a buttery pale yellow interior. The flavor has a mild burnt tinge to it.

Silter (SIHL-tehr) A semi-hard, cow's milk cheese coming from the province of Brescia, in the region of Lombardy. It has a brown-yellow interior and mild taste.

Spressa delle Giudicarie (SPREH-sah DEHL-leh joo-dee-KAHR-ee-eh) (**PDO 2003**) A semi-hard, cow's milk cheese made in the region of Trentino-Alto Adige. It is cylindrical in shape with a light straw-colored exterior and bears the mark *Spressa*. The interior is pale yellow with many holes.

Squacquerone di Romagna (skwah-kweh-OH-neh dee roh-MAHN-yah) (**PDO 2012**) A round, cow's milk cheese made in the region of Emilia-Romagna. It is an ancient cheese dating back to the early 1800s. It is rindless with a pure white exterior, with markings from the plastic tub it was made in. The interior is white and soft, with a pleasant, slightly salty taste. The cheese is typically spread on *Piadina* bread (flat bread) made in the region.

Stelvio (STEHL-vee-oh) (**PDO 2007**) A cylindrical-shaped, cow's milk cheese from the Stelvio Valley, in the region of Trentino-Alto Adige. This cheese has been made for hundreds of years but only recognized and called Stelvio in 1914. It has a yellow-orange to orange-brown exterior. The interior, which is semisoft, ranges from pale yellow to straw yellow with irregular small to medium large holes. Also known as *Stilfser* (Germany).

Stracchino (strah-KEE-noh) A generic term applied to cheeses, which since around 1100 A.D., have been made in the plains of Lombardy from cow's milk. Stracchino is derived from the Lombard dialect word *stracca*, meaning "tired" supposedly, from tired cow's moving seasonally up and down the Alps. Stracchino is a rindless cheese with a dry, beige exterior and a delicate, soft creamy texture with a somewhat acidic taste. Some examples of stracchino cheese are Certosa (Lombardy), Crescenza (Lombardy, Piedmont, Veneto), and Gorgonzola (Lombardy). <u>Recommended Beverages</u>: **White:** Friulano, Pinot Blanc, Pinot Grigio, Soave, Verdicchio; **Red:** Pinot Noir.

T

Taleggio (tah-LEHD-joh) (***PDO 1996***)
- _Similar To_: Quartirolo Lombardo
- _Region Of Origin_: In the Taleggio Valley, in the province of Bergamo, Lombardy; Piedmont, and Veneto
- _History_: It has been produced since the tenth century
- _Type Of Milk_: Cow
- _Appearance And Shape_: Yellow-tan exterior with inedible rind; pale yellow interior with some holes; Square-shaped
- _Texture_: Semisoft, smooth, silky, and buttery
- _Aroma And Flavor_: Nutty and tangy flavor that sharpens with age
- _Recommended Beverages_: **Red**: Amarone della Valpolicella, Bardolino, Beaujolais, Cabernet Sauvignon, Dolcetto, Grignolino, Merlot, Montefalco Sagrantino, Nebbiolo, Pinot Noir, Sangiovese, Valpolicella, Zinfandel; **White**: Chardonnay, Chenin Blanc, Cortese, Orvieto, Riesling, Sauvignon Blanc, Soave: **Other**: Sherry (semisweet); Vin Santo

Toma (TOH-mah) A generic name for a group of cheeses made in Piedmont, Valle d'Aosta, and Lombardy, from predominately cow's milk, which varies from locale to locale, each with its own special character. Most are soft to semisoft in texture and generally not meant to be aged. They are usually eaten after a meal, drizzled with olive oil, salt and pepper. When aged, the rind is rough and the yellow interior is dense with a sharp, salty taste.

The word Toma is derived from one of the steps in making the cheese, *tuma* being a dialect word for fall or precipitation of the casein during coagulation of the milk. The most widely known are *Toma del Biellese* (Piedmont), *Toma della Val di Susa* (Piedmont), *Toma della Valle Viona* (Piedmont), *Toma di Battelmatt*, *Toma di Boves* (Piedmont), *Toma di Lanzo* (Piedmont), *Toma Grassa* (Piedmont), *Toma Magra* (Piedmont), *Toma Piemontese,* and *Toma Semigrassa* (Piedmont). The smaller version is called *Tomini*. It is similar to *Paglia*. Also known as *Tuma*. *See* Tometta. <u>Recommended Beverages</u>: Barbera, Bardolino, Dolcetto, Grignolino, Merlot, Nebbiolo, Sangiovese, and Valpolicella.

Toma Piemontese (TOH-mah pyeh-mohn-TEH-zeh) (**PDO 1996**) A semi-hard, cow's cheese made in the region of Piedmont. It is cylindrical-shaped, with a pale yellow to brownish rustic rind that accrues mold with age. The interior is straw-colored with a few small holes. The cheese develops a nutty flavor as it ages. *See* Toma.

Tometta (toh-MEHT-tah) A cylindrical-shaped, cow's milk cheese from Piedmont. There are many kinds of Tometta cheese, among them: *Tometta della Val Chiusella, Tometta di Barge, Tometta di Castellamonte,* and *Tometta di Quincinetto. See* Toma.

Tomini (toh-MEE-nee) A soft and crumbly, disk-shaped, cow's (occasionally goat) milk cheese from Piedmont, with a white, rindless exterior and delicate, slightly acidic and pleasant flavor. It is often preserved in pepper and makes an excellent antipasto cheese. *See* Toma.

V

Vacchino Romano (VAHK-kee-noh roh-MAHN-oh) A hard, grana-type, cow's milk cheese made in Latium. *See* Grana.

Valle d'Aosta Fromadzo (VAHL-leh DOHS-tah froh-MAHD-zoh) (**PDO 1996**) A cylindrical-shaped cow's milk cheese made in the region of Valle d'Aosta. Its exterior is pale yellow to gray, changing to reddish tones with age. The interior is pale yellow scattered with small to medium-holes. A lightly salty taste with a hint of spicy if mature and has a pleasant smell of milk and aromatic mountain herbs. The cheese can also be flavored with juniper berries, cumin, or wild fennel.

Valtellina Casera (vahl-tehl-LEE-nah kah-SEHR-ah) (**PDO 1996**) A cylindrical-shaped, semi-firm, cow's milk cheese made in the province of Sondrio, Lombardy. It has a pale colored exterior and interior, with an uneven scattering of small holes. Its flavor is nutty and become tangy with age. Its origins date back to the sixteenth century and is used much in the cuisine of Valtellina.

Vastedda della Valle del Belìce (vahs-TEHD-dah DEHL-lah VAHL-leh dehl beh-LEE-cheh) (***PDO 2010***) A round, fresh sheep's milk cheese made in Sicily. It is typically eaten within three days of production. The cheese is pure white in color, with a slightly sour taste, but not spicy.

Vezzena (vetz-ZEH-nah)
- _Similar To_: Asiago
- _Region Of Origin_: Trentino-Alto Adige
- _History_: It is made high up in the area around Mount Vezzena.
- _Type Of Milk_: Cow
- _Appearance And Shape_: Dark oily exterior; dull yellow interior with no holes; round-shaped
- _Texture_: Hard and granular
- _Aroma And Flavor_: Sharp flavor to the point of bitterness
- _Comments_: It is generally aged six months to one year, depending on whether it is to be used as a table or grating cheese.
- _Recommended Beverages_: _See_ Asiago

Italian Wines (And Other Beverages) "A - Z"

Although there are more than 8,000 grape varieties in the world, most of them are not suitable for making fine wine, nor are their parent grapevine species highly regarded. An attempt to provide a comprehensive description of all these grape varieties and the wines they make is a monumental undertaking. Therefore, only the most prominent grapes and wines they make are covered.

Aglianico (ahl-YAHN-ee-koh)

- _Background_: (_Italy_) A thick-skinned, high acid, very dark red grape variety, which according to legend, ancient Greek settlers around 800 B.C brought the Aglianico grape to Italy. However, there is no evidence to support that hypothesis. The name Aglianico was first used in a letter dated 1559, from Sante Lancerio, cellarmaster to Pope Paul III, to Cardinal Guido Ascanio Sforza (Pope's nephew). Lancerio wrote, "Aglianico wine comes from the Kingdom of Naples, where they make a good Greco." The Aglianico grape is grown mostly in southern Italy; Apulia, Calabria, and Molise, but really flourishes in Basilicata and Campania.
- _Bouquet & Flavor_: Intense ruby-red color, distinctive complex fragrance and flavor of berries (blackberry, strawberry),

cherries, red licorice, and plums, with nuances of bitter chocolate, black pepper, coffee, leather, tobacco, violets, and earthi-
ness. Powerful and broadly structured with firm tannins and a
long finish.

- _Recommended Cheeses_: Asiago, Bagozzo, Blue Cheeses,
Caciocavallo, Fiore Sardo, Gorgonzola, Grana, Parmigiano-
Reggiano, Pecorino, and Provolone.

Amarone della Valpolicella (ah-mah-ROH-neh DEHL-lah vahl-poh-lee-CHEHL-lah)

- _Background_: (_Italy_) A wine produced on hilly portions of the
Valpolicella Classico Zone in the northeastern part of Veneto,
bordered on the west by the Adige River. The word _amarone_
comes from the Veronese dialect; it means "bone dry" almost to the point of bitterness. The grapes used are Corvina
Veronese, Corvinone, and Rondinella, with the possible addition of Molinara, Croatina, Dindarella, Forselina, Negrara,
Oseleta, Sangiovese, Teroldego, Cabernet Franc, Cabernet
Sauvignon, and Merlot. Amarone, however, unlike Valpolicella,
is made exclusively from the best grapes, which are located at
the top and outside perimeter of the clusters. The grapes used
for Amarone are grown on three-foot-high trellises in the hills
of Valpolicella that rise one to two thousand feet above sea level. The best grapes, those that receive the most direct sunshine,
are called _recie_ or _orecchie_ (ears), hence the formerly used name
Recioto della Valpolicella Amarone (_recioto_ is a word from the
old Veronese dialect of the area).
- In the picking process, more than 50 percent (officially up to a
maximum of 70 percent) of the grapes are immediately reject-
ed because they are not ripe enough. In addition, the selected
bunches are those whose grapes are sufficiently spaced to allow
air to circulate between in the eventual drying process (this
limits the formation of _grey mold_). These grapes, whose sugar

levels are the highest due to the amount of sunlight they receive, are picked and then arranged on flat, mostly plastic drawers, called *tavoloni*, which easily fit into racks (called *arelle*), which allow a good circulation of air. It is very important they be kept in a dry, cool, well-ventilated room, so fans and dehumidifiers are often used. A few producers have created temperature and humidity-controlled *drying rooms* for dehydrating the grapes. In years past, bamboo, straw mats, or vertical trellises were used to dry the grapes. Each drawer is clearly marked with the day the grapes were picked and the part of the vineyard from which they originate. The grapes are cleaned and turned about every 20 days and are constantly inspected during the three- to four-month drying period. This drying period (known as *appassimento* or resting period) causes a 30 percent loss of juice, with a resulting high level of sugar and varietal character, without a corresponding increase in acidity. The concentrated fruit extract of the grapes is what some mistake for sweetness. Most Amarone winemakers believe that *Botrytis cinerea* is a drawback and discourage its formation on Corvina and other grapes. *Botrytis*, which releases glucuronic acid, also increases oxidation, and sometimes off-flavors. Enzymatic action also changes the properties of the acids and sugar balance. The dried, shriveled grapes are pressed late February or early March and fermented slowly for approximately 45 days with the skins, and occasionally stems intact. The wine is aged for a minimum of two years (*DOCG* regulations) in wood, but it is not uncommon for Amarone to be aged for five years or more in barrels prior to bottling and further bottle aging.

- The resultant wine is, not surprisingly, highly alcoholic: a minimum of 14 percent under *DOCG* law. However, most Amarone wines are even higher in alcohol, sometimes as high as 17 percent. When produced in the heart of the *DOCG* production zone the wine may be labeled *classico*. Amarone received its *DOC* status in 1968 and was elevated to *DOCG* in 2010. Formerly known as Recioto della Valpolicella Amarone.

- *Bouquet & Flavor*: Darkish ruby red color. Lush, persistent spicy bouquet of sweet cherry, roses; almost port-like. A moderately robust, strong, concentrated, complex flavor of dried fruit, reminiscent of bitter almonds, cherries, chestnuts, cinnamon, coffee, figs, hawthorn, hazelnuts, licorice, peaches, dried plums, raisins, tobacco, violets, walnuts, and wild berries with considerable finesse, and velvety rich. The aftertaste is warming, slightly bitter, and quite dry, with sensations of rich spicy fruit.
- *Recommended Cheeses*: Aostino, Asiago, Bagozzo, Bitto, Fiore Sardo, Gorgonzola, Grana, Parmigiano-Reggiano, Pecorino, Provolone, and Taleggio.

Asti (AHS-tee)

- *Background*: (*Italy*): A *DOCG* (1993) white, sweet sparkling wine produced in the southern area of Langhe (province of Cuneo) and Monferrato (province of Asti and Alessandria), in the Piedmont region. The production area was delimited on March 7, 1924, when *Asti Spumante* was classified as a *typical wine*. When the *DOCG* was granted, with it came a name change to *Asti* with the suffix *Spumante* deleted. Asti is made from 100 percent Moscato Bianco grapes.
- *Bouquet & Flavor*: Light straw-yellow or golden-yellow in color with a delicate, musky, and spicy aroma that is reminiscent of apricots, orange blossoms, peaches, and pears. Also present is the seductive scent of wild honey, linden leaves, acacia blossoms, wisteria, and sage. It is sweet and harmonious, tasting very much of the Moscato grape, with balanced acidity and a long and lingering aftertaste.
- *Recommended Cheeses*: *See* Champagne and Sparkling Wine (Semisweet to Sweet)

Barbera (bahr-BEHR-ah)

- _Background_: (*Italy*) A thin-skinned, high acid, red grape variety grown primarily in Piedmont, and in small quantities in many other countries, most notably California, U.S.A. Although its exact origins are uncertain, it is believed to have originated from a spontaneous crossing of seeds from ancient grapevines growing in the hilly area known as Monferrato in southern Piedmont; in fact, its ampelographical name is *Vitis vinifera Montisferratensis*. The name Barbera was first mentioned in a land register from Chieri in 1514 in Piedmont, and was supposedly introduced in the province of Cuneo in 1685, by Count Cotti of Neive.
- _Bouquet & Flavor_: Deep brilliant ruby color. Bouquet and flavors of berries (blackberry, boysenberry, cranberry, raspberry); black cherry, black figs, red currant chamomile, cinnamon, clove, earthy, herbs, licorice, nutmeg, pepper, dried plums, roses, tobacco, tomato, and violets. Medium-bodied with a naturally high level of acidity and a tart-berry aftertaste.
- _Recommended Cheeses_: Asiago, Bagozzo, Bel Paese, Blue Cheeses, Bra, Caciocavallo, Fiore Sardo, Fontina, Gorgonzola, Grana, Parmigiano-Reggiano, Pecorino, Provolone, Ricotta, and Toma.

Bardolino (bahr-doh-LEE-noh)

- _Background_: (*Italy*) A DOC (1968) red wine produced in the northeastern region of Veneto. From the Brenner-Verona highway, the classico zone of Bardolino can be seen in the rolling hills between the Adige and Lake Garda. Bardolino is produced in the area southeast of Lake Garda, including all or parts of the communal territories of Bardolino, Garda, and others, in the province of Verona. The name *Bardolino* is relatively recent; in the early part of the 1900s, it was called *Garda wine*, although the wine itself is very old indeed.

- Bardolino is made from Corvina Veronese and Rondinella grapes, with lesser amounts of Rossignola, Barbera, Sangiovese, Marzemino, Merlot, and Cabernet Sauvignon.
- Bardolino Classico must come from a strictly delimited area of production in the fertile, glacial moraine hills of La Garda. There is also a very light Bardolino, resembling a rosé, called Bardolino *Chiaretto*. Bardolino bottled by December 31 of the year of the harvest can be identified on the label as *novello* (nouveau). The consorzio of Bardolino features a Roman arena at Verona on its neck label.
- Since 2001, there is a *DOCG* Bardolino *Superiore* and *Classico Superiore*.
- *Bouquet & Flavor*: Bright ruby-red in color, tending at times to be cherry red. It has a light and delicate aroma, reminiscent of candy-apple, cherries, cranberry, and raspberries. It has a dry, spicy cherry and fruity taste, with a good balance, subtle, and at times a lightly spritzy flavor.
- *Recommended Cheeses*: Asiago, Bagozzo, Bel Paese, Blue Cheeses, Burrata, Burrini, Caciocavallo, Fontina, Grana, Mozzarella, Parmigiano-Reggiano, Pecorino, Provolone, Ricotta, Robiola Piemonte, Scamorza, Taleggio, and Toma.

Beer (Dark)
- *Background*: A beer characterized by a very deep, dark color, full-bodied flavor, and a creamy taste, with overtones of malt, bitterness, sweetness, and caramel. Its usual production involves the addition of roasted barley during the initial brewing stages.
- *Recommended Cheeses*: Blue Cheeses

Bourbon and Tennessee Whiskey
- Background: Bourbon whiskey is a distinctive whiskey of Kentucky (although it can be produced anywhere in the United States), made predominantly from corn. Federal regulations

require that bourbon whiskey be made from a minimum of 51 percent corn; however, 65 to 75 percent is generally used. When the corn in the mash reaches 80 percent, the product, by government definition, becomes corn whiskey—not bourbon. The higher the corn content and the lower the percentage of other grains, the lighter the whiskey. The blend of the other grains is dictated by the distiller's own private formula; rye, wheat, or barley can be used in the grain mix.

- Federal law (1935) specifies that Bourbon must be distilled at no higher than 160 proof. It must be stored at no less than 80 proof and not more than 125 proof in new, charred white oak barrels ranging in capacity from 50 to 66 gallons, for a minimum of two years (to be labeled *Straight Bourbon Whiskey*), although most distillers age their bourbon anywhere from four to ten years. Although Straight Bourbon Whiskey must be aged a minimum of two years, if it is released prior to the fourth year of aging, it must be stated on the label. In addition, no coloring or flavoring can be added. Only distilled water may be added to the Bourbon before bottling, to achieve the proper bottling proof, which must be at least 80 proof.

- Tennessee Whiskey is a proprietary whiskey from the state of Tennessee that is double distilled at not exceeding 160 proof from a fermented mash of not less than 51 percent corn, with the remaining grains being barley, oats, rye, and wheat. Tennessee whiskey is leached or filtered through vats, containing ten feet of compacted sugar maple charcoal, which eliminates congeners and adds to its flavor prior to being aged in new, charred American oak barrels.

- <u>*Recommended Cheeses*</u>: Asiago, Bagozzo, Grana, Parmigiano-Reggiano, and Pecorino.

Brachetto d'Acqui (brah-KEHT-toh DAH-kwee)

- <u>*Background*</u>: (*Italy*): A *DOCG* (1996) red sweet wine made in the provinces of Alessandria and Asti in the Piedmont region. It is made principally from Brachetto grapes. A *spumante* and *passito* styles are authorized.

- *Bouquet & Flavor:* Aromas and flavors of ripe fruit, roses, strawberries, violets; jammy-fruit aroma; off-dry grapey flavors, good acidic, sweet finish with a touch of grassiness.
- *Recommended Cheeses*: *See* Champagne and Sparkling Wine (Semisweet to Sweet)

Brandy (Fruit)

- *Background*: Fruit brandies may be produced from almost any kind of fruit. Wild or cultivated fruits containing stones or seeds, and even most berries, will yield a suitable-tasting brandy. The brandy may also be aged in oak barrels. Fruit brandies are dry, usually colorless, and generally high proof. Fruit brandies state on their labels the name of the fruit used, or use accepted European names. Some examples are—*Airelle, Alisier, Apfelschnaps, Applejack* or *apple brandy, Barack Pálinka* (Austria and Hungary), *Batzi* (Switzerland), *Birnengeist, Calvados, Coing, Császarkorte, Fraise, Framboise, Groseille, Himbeergeist, Houx, Kirsch, Kirschwasser, Marillenbrand, Medronho (madroño), Mirabelle, Mûre, Myrtille, Nèfle, Nezhinskaya Ryafina, Pálinka* (Austria and Hungary), *Pêche, Pflümli, Poire, Pomme, Prunelle, Prunelle Sauvage, Quetsch, Reine-Claude, Sargadoz, Schwarzwälder, Slivovitz, Sorbier, Sureau,* and *Zwetschgenwasser.*
- *Recommended Cheeses*: Blue Cheeses and Triple-Crèmes.

Brandy (Grapes)

- *Background*: A spirit made by distilling (less than 190 proof) wines or the fermented mash of fruit, which then may or may not be aged in oak barrels. The varying characteristics of different brandies are the result of differences in fruit and grape varieties, climate, soil, and production methods, which vary from district to district and country to country. To be simply labeled as *brandy*, the product must have been made solely from grapes. If other fruits are used, the label must indicate what fruits they are, such as apple brandy, cherry brandy, and so forth.

- The name brandy originates with the Dutch, who are believed to have been the first great connoisseurs of this drink; they called it *brandewijn*, meaning burnt wine. This referred to the process by which brandy was made: wine was heated and the resulting vapor distilled. This term was carried over into Germany as *branntwein* (weinbrand) and into France as *brandevin*. The English adopted the word as brandywine, which was later shortened to brandy.

- <u>*Recommended Cheeses*</u>: Blue Cheeses, Gorgonzola, and Triple-Crèmes.

Cabernet Sauvignon (kah-behr-NAY soh-veen-YOHN)

- <u>*Background*</u>: A thick-skinned, major red grape variety acknowledged worldwide as producing some of the finest dry red wines and is often referred to as the noblest of all red grape varieties. In France, it is grown principally in the Bordeaux region, although planted in other regions as well.

- In 1997, Carole Meredith, a professor of enology and viticulture at the University of California at Davis, revealed Cabernet Sauvignon's parentage through DNA testing. She stated that it is "150 trillion times" more likely that Cabernet Franc and Sauvignon Blanc– rather than any other varieties– were responsible for the cross-pollination leading to Cabernet Sauvignon's appearance in the late seventeenth century. Meredith believes Cabernet Sauvignon's creation was an accident of nature, because, she says, its use as a wine grape predates recorded human experimentation with plant hybridization. Because cuttings rather than seeds traditionally propagate grapevines, it is conceivable that the entire world's Cabernet Sauvignon vineyards spring from one original plant. Cabernet Sauvignon berries are quite small with a high ration of pits and skin to pulp.

- Around 1860, Almadén Vineyards produced California's first commercial Cabernet Sauvignon.
- *Bouquet & Flavor*: *Cabernet Sauvignon*. It covers a wide spectrum of aromas and flavors. It tends towards herbaceous when not fully ripe with capsicum and grassy undertones. When ripe, aromas and flavors of asparagus, bell pepper, berries (blackberry, blueberry, cranberry, raspberry), black or green olives, black cherry, black currants, black tea, celery, chocolate, dill, eucalyptus, licorice, molasses, mint, plum, prune, rhubarb, soy, and various herbs. **Aromas and Flavors from oak:** Cedar, coffee, leather, musk, sandalwood, smoke, toast, tobacco, vanilla, and spicy notes.
- *Recommended Cheeses*: Asiago, Bagozzo, Blue Cheeses, Burrata, Burrini, Caciocavallo, Caciotta, Fiore Sardo, Gorgonzola, Grana, Mozzarella, Parmigiano-Reggiano, Pecorino, Pressato, Provolone, Scamorza, Taleggio, and Triple-Crèmes

Carmenère (kahr-mehn-YEHR)
- *Background*: A thick-skinned, low acid, red grape variety, which flourished in Bordeaux, France prior to the outbreak of phylloxera during the 1870s. Its name is supposedly derived from the word *carmine*, an obvious reference to its deep, rich color. There is less than 500 acres planted in all of Bordeaux, although it is grown in Chile, Italy, and China.
- *Bouquet & Flavor*: Bright cherry-colored with an aroma and flavor of berries (blackberry, cranberry, raspberry), black cherries, black currants, black olives, black pepper, green pepper, black tea, chocolate, coffee, dried plums, and tart-berries. Also present are hints of cedar, herbs, leather, mint, spices, and tobacco.
- *Recommended Cheeses*: Blue Cheeses and Fontina

Catarratto (kah-tah-RAH-toh)
- *Background*: A low acid, white grape variety grown principally in Sicily, where it is used mostly as a blending grape and also in

Marsala wine. Two of its clones are known as *Catarratto Comune* and *Catarratto Lucido*. Catarratto is also grown in Tunisia and California.
- *Bouquet & Flavor*: Straw-colored with green highlights; a perfumed-earthy bouquet and taste of apples, citrus, figs, grass, green olives, honeysuckle, melon, nuts, peaches, and pears. Medium-bodied, dry and clean with mineral-like flavors, lemon oil, wild herbs and a bitter-almond aftertaste.
- *Recommended Cheeses*: Pecorino

Champagne and Sparkling Wine (Dry)
- *Bouquet & Flavor*: (GENERIC) Red and green apples, pears, biscuit pastry, fresh butter, ripe wheat, spices, tobacco, truffles, violets; citrus to toasty, nutty tones.
- See Franciacorta and Prosecco
- *Recommended Cheeses*: Asiago, Bagozzo, Blue Cheeses, Fontina, Grana, Parmigiano-Reggiano, Pecorino, Pressato, and Triple-Crèmes.

Champagne and Sparkling Wine (Semisweet to Sweet)
- *Bouquet & Flavor*: See Asti and Brachetto d'Acqui
- *Recommended Cheeses*: Aostino, Gorgonzola, and Ricotta

Chardonnay (shahr-doh-NAY)
- *Background*: A thin-skinned, medium acid, white grape variety acknowledged worldwide as producing some of the finest dry white wines. It is grown extensively in Burgundy and Champagne, France, as well as in most other wine-producing countries of the world. In 1936, Wente Vineyards of California was the first winery to bottle Chardonnay as a separate varietal.
- In 1999, Carole Meredith, a professor of enology and viticulture at the University of California at Davis, revealed Chardonnay's parentage through DNA testing. Genetic testing has proven

that Chardonnay is the offspring of the noble Pinot family and Gouais Blanc, a variety so obscure that cuttings could only be obtained from the agricultural archives in France. The evidence does not specify whether Pinot Noir, Pinot Gris, or Pinot Blanc was Chardonnay's progenitor. Current DNA technology cannot differentiate between the three. Pinot Noir may be the most likely candidate, according to Meredith, because it has always been the most common in France.

- There is a small village named Chardonnay, which is nestled among the vineyards, close to the celebrated Romanesque church of Tournus in Burgundy. No one, however, can establish whether the village was named after the grape, or vice versa. Chardonnay was formerly known as *Pinot Chardonnay* although as long ago as 1872, a group of French scientists from Lyon, Burgundy, France, determined that Chardonnay was a non-Pinot variety.

- *Bouquet & Flavor*: Ranges from pale yellow to medium gold in color, depending on the length of time the wine was aged in both the barrel and bottle. Chardonnay exhibits some of the following aroma and taste characteristics: Acacia, apples (sometimes green apple), apricot, asparagus, banana, celery, citrus (grapefruit, lemon), figs, guava, hawthorn, mango, melon, orange, papaya, peaches, pears, pineapples, quince, sage, and sweet cooked-apple.

- If Chardonnay undergoes *malolactic fermentation* the smell and flavor of butter and cheese rind is present

- If barrel-fermented or aged in wood, overtones of butterscotch, brown sugar, caramel, clove, coconut, coffee, hazelnut, honey, fresh wood, molasses, nutmeg, smoke, spice, toasted bread, vanilla.

- *Recommended Cheeses*: Asiago, Bagozzo, Bel Paese, Blue Cheeses, Burrata, Burrini, Caciocavallo, Fontina, Grana, Mozzarella, Parmigiano-Reggiano, Pecorino, Provolone, Ricotta, Scamorza, Taleggio, and Triple-Crèmes.

Chenin Blanc (shuh-NAHN blahn)

- *Background*: A thin-skinned, high acid, white grape variety grown worldwide and especially in Bordeaux and the Loire Valley of France. Chenin Blanc can be vinified into a dry, semidry, sweet, or even sparkling wine. Chenin Blanc is known to be have been growing in the year 845, on the left bank of the Loire River in Anjou at the Abbey of Glanfeuil. Its present name dates back from around the fifteenth century from the monastery of Mont-Chenin in the Touraine district and it is cited by name in the literature of Rabelais.

- In 1954, the Charles Krug Winery of Napa Valley, California, was the first winery to offer Chenin Blanc as a separate variety.

- *Bouquet & Flavor*: Chenin Blanc can be vinified into a dry, semidry, sweet, or even sparkling wine. Aromas and flavors of red apple, apricot, banana, celery, chamomile, curry, fresh fruit salad, grass, guava, honeysuckle, lemon, melon, orange peel, peach, pear, pineapple, pumpkin, quince, strawberry, tangerine, tropical fruit, and wet wool.

- *Recommended Cheeses*: Aostino, Bel Paese, Burrata, Burrini, Mozzarella, Ricotta, Scamorza, Taleggio, and Triple-Crèmes.

Cortese (kohr-TEH-zeh)

- *Background*: (*Italy*) A medium acid, white grape variety of Piedmont (also some in Lombardy and Veneto). It is believed to be first mentioned in print as early as 1614. Once widely grown throughout southern Piedmont, its area of production is now limited to the provinces of Asti and Alessandria.

- *Bouquet & Flavor*: Pale straw in color with a green hue. It has an aroma and flavor of green apples, apricots, chamomile, citrus (grapefruit, lemon, orange), honey, melons, peaches, pears, and tropical fruit. It has hints of lily of the valley, with a crisp finish and lingering, bitter-almond aftertaste.

- _Recommended Cheeses_: Asiago, Bagozzo, Bitto, Blue Cheeses, Caciocavallo, Fontina, Grana, Parmigiano-Reggiano, Pecorino, Robiola Piemonte, Taleggio, and Triple-Crèmes.

Dolcetto (dohl-CHEHT-toh)

- _Background_: (_Italy_) A red grape variety, rich in pigment and low in acidity, grown principally in the Piedmont region, where it is produced in the Langhe Hills just south of the town of Alba. Some is also grown in Liguria and Valle d'Aosta. The Dolcetto grapevine is indigenous to the area and was subject to local government regulations as early as 1593. Count Nuvolone, who referred to by one of its synonyms…Dosset, first mentioned it in print in 1799.
- The name Dolcetto could be roughly translated to mean _little sweet one_. The name, however, is misleading: Dolcetto is a dry red wine with a pleasing bitter aftertaste.
- _Bouquet & Flavor_: Deep purple color; intensely fruity with a bouquet of berries (blackberry, raspberry), cherries, chocolate, chestnuts, jam, porcini mushrooms, plums, and quince. Dry and pleasant, with scents of almonds, coffee, licorice, and spice, with a soft, pleasing bitter aftertaste.
- _Recommended Cheeses_: Asiago, Bagozzo, Blue Cheeses, Burrata, Burrini, Fontina, Gorgonzola, Grana, Montasio, Mozzarella, Parmigiano-Reggiano, Pecorino, Provolone, Ricotta, Robiola Piemonte, Scamorza, Taleggio, and Toma.

Fiano (fee-AH-noh)

- _Background_: (_Italy_) A white grape variety grown primarily in the region of Campania since at the least the 1200s. Fiano is also grown in Sicily, Apulia, Basilicata, Marches, and Molise; and in Australia.
- _Bouquet & Flavor_: _Fiano_. Straw-yellow color; aromas of lavender, along with flavors of apple, apricot, citrus (lime), hazelnut,

honey, pear, pine nuts, pineapple, and spices, with a pleasing bitter finish.

- *Recommended Cheeses*: Asiago, Bagozzo, Fiore Sardo, Grana, Parmigiano-Reggiano, and Pecorino.

Franciacorta (frahn-chah-KOHR-tah)

- *Background*: (*Italy*): A *DOC* (1995) [Note: The Curtefranca *DOC* was created in 1995 as Terre di Franciacorta *DOC*. In 2008 the name was changed to Curtefranca *DOC*] for red and white wines produced in the province of Brescia in the Lombardy region. Red grapes include Cabernet Franc, Carmenère, Cabernet Sauvignon, Merlot, and Pinot Noir. White grapes include Chardonnay and Pinot Bianco.
- *Bouquet & Flavor*: Straw yellow with greenish or golden hues, fine and persistent pin-point bubbles, bouquet with a hints of almonds, apples, bread crust, citrus, dried fruit, figs, hazelnuts, pears, wheat, and dried flowers.
- *Recommended Cheeses*: *See* Champagne and Sparkling Wine (Dry)

Frascati (frahs-KAH-tee)

- *Background*: (*Italy*) A *DOC* (1966) white wine produced around the village of Frascati, on the slopes of the Alban hills in the Castelli Romani district, south of Rome in the Latium region. The name Frascati comes from the *frasche* (branches), which the inhabitants used to build huts for shelter.
- It is made principally from Malvasia (Bianca di Candia and del Lazio) grapes, with lesser amounts Bellone, Trebbiano (Toscano and Giallo), Bombino Bianco, and Greco. A *spumante* style is authorized.
- *Bouquet & Flavor*: Pale straw in color with a clean, fresh, fruity aroma of apples, citrus (lemon), pears, and tropical fruits. It is

soft and fruity tasting with a dry finish and a lingering, faint almond aftertaste.

- *Recommended Cheeses*: Bel Paese, Burrata, Burrini, Caprini, Mozzarella, Ricotta, and Scamorza.

Friulano (Tocai) (free-oo-LAH-noh)

- *Background*: (*Italy*) A white grape variety grown in the Italian regions of Friuli-Venezia Giulia, Lombardy, Tuscany, and Veneto, as well as in California, Argentina, and Chile.
- In the 1950s, the Hungarian Government attempted to stop Italian use of the name Tocai, arguing that Hungarian Tokay was the original. In 1954, after extensive studies by a panel of experts, an International Court in Trieste decided that Hungary did not have exclusive rights to the name Tocai and that the Hungarian grape Furmint (used to make Tokay) is a different grape variety entirely. According to the panel's findings, both of these grapevines actually originated in Italy. It is believed that the Italian missionaries to the court of King Steven I (997–1038), brought them to Hungary in the eleventh century. Under a 1993 accord with Hungary, France agreed to stop labeling their wines *Tokay* made from the Pinot Gris grape in Alsace, while Italy would refrain from labeling their wines *Tocai*, a grape variety grown in the Friuli-Venezia Giulia region. The agreement took effect March 2007. Wine made from the Tocai grape is now known as *Friulano*.
- *Bouquet & Flavor*: Light yellow with some green hints. Aroma and flavor of almonds, apple, citrus, mace, minerals, nutmeg, peaches, pears, wild flowers, and hay, with a pleasing, bitter aftertaste.
- *Recommended Cheeses*: Asiago, Bagozzo, Bernardo, Fontina, Gorgonzola, Grana, Parmigiano-Reggiano, Pecorino, Provolone, and Stracchino.

Gamay (gah-MAY)

- _Background_: (_France_) A thick-skinned, red grape variety of the Beaujolais district of France. On July 31, 1394, Philippe le Hardi (the Bold), Duke of Burgundy (1364–1404), issued an edict banishing the "evil and disloyal" Gamay grape from his kingdom (the areas around Dijon, Beaune, and Chalon) in favor of the bigger and fruitier Pinot Noir grape, which was in demand at that time. In the ten Beaujolais _crus_, it is capable of making a more serious, age worthy red. In addition to France, the Gamay grape is grown in most wine-producing countries of the world.
- _Bouquet & Flavor_: Extremely fruity, berrylike (blackberry, cranberry, raspberry, strawberry), and cherry, with aromas and flavors of bubblegum, banana, cinnamon, and mint.
- _Recommended Cheeses_: Bel Paese, Blue Cheeses, Burrata, Burrini, Fontina, Mozzarella, Scamorza, Taleggio, and Triple-Crèmes.

Gewürztraminer (geh-VERTS-trah-MEE-nehr)

- _Background_: A thick-skinned, low acid, white grape variety with a slightly pinkish skin, believed to be originally from the Pfalz region of Germany, although increasingly it is speculated that it was first grown around 1000 A.D. in the village of Tramin (_Traminer_ "from Tramin"); _Termeno_ in Italian, in the province of Bolzano, in Southern Tyrol of the Trentino-Alto Adige region. In Germany, the name _Gewürz_ means _spicy_. In the late nineteenth century, Alsatians began calling this grapevine Gewürztraminer, but it wasn't until 1973 that name was officially sanctioned and the name _Traminer_ was discontinued in Alsace except for in the Heiligenstein area. Gewürztraminer is grown in most regions of the world although it is quintessentially an Alsatian wine and very few if any countries produce a wine of equal distinction.
- In Italy, Gewürztraminer is known as _Traminer Aromatico_.

- *Bouquet & Flavor*: Delicious, spicy, and fruity, with a pungent flavor and a highly perfumed and flowery bouquet that is strongly reminiscent of apple, apricot, citrus (grapefruit, lemon), ginger, honeysuckle, litchi, mango, melon, orange, peach, pineapple, quince, rose petals, spices (allspice, cinnamon), and a tropical fruit salad. Its aroma is often assertive on the palate, finishing with a touch of bitterness. Gewürztraminer can range from very dry, semisweet, to extremely sweet, and even sparkling.
- *Recommended Cheeses*: Asiago, Bagozzo, Bernardo, Blue Cheeses, Fontina, Gorgonzola, Grana, Mozzarella, Parmigiano-Reggiano, Pecorino, Provolone, Ricotta, Scamorza, and Triple-Crèmes.

Grappa (GRAHP-pah)
- *Background*: (*Italy*) Grappa is a distillate made principally from the skins, pulp, and seeds (collectively known as *pomace* or *vinaccia* in Italian) of grapes—the remains from the pressing of the grapes for winemaking. Most grappa is not aged in wooden barrels, but rather in stainless steel or glass containers. In Italy, grappa is made by distillers collectively known as *grappaioli*.
- The origin of the name *grappa* comes from a commune called *Bassano del Grappa* northeast of Verona in the Veneto region of Italy, where grappa has been produced since 1451. Northern Italy accounts for approximately 90 percent of the grappa sold in Italy.
- *Bouquet & Flavor*: Grappa is usually clear or faintly amber in color, with a fruity bouquet reminiscent of the natural nuances of the different woods occasionally used to age it. Its taste is round, soft, herbal, fruity, spicy, and peppery, with scents of dry flowers and leaves.
- *Recommended Cheeses*: Gorgonzola

Greco (GREH-koh)

- _Background_: (_Italy_) A variety of ancient white grapes widely cultivated mostly in Southern Italy. The grape is thought to have brought from Greece around 800 B.C., when they were colonizing the central and southern part of Italy. On the label, it normally appears with the name of the town or region of production. Some is also grown in Apulia, Basilicata, Calabria, Latium, Molise, and Umbria. The better-known examples are _Greco di Ancona_ and _Greco di Tufo_.
- _Bouquet & Flavor_: Delicate scents of ripe apricots, apples, fern and mint, with a pleasing bitter almond finish.
- _Recommended Cheeses_: Caciocavallo, Calcagno, Fiore Sardo, and Provolone.

Grenache (greh-NAHSH)

- _Background_: (_Spain_) A thin-skinned, medium acid, red grape variety of Spanish origins, which was brought to France sometime in the Middle Ages. In the United States it is used mainly as a blending grape or used to make rosé wines. It is widely grown throughout the Mediterranean, especially in France's Rhône region, where it is blended along with Syrah to make most of its red wines—and some rosé wines. In Spain, it produces the red wines from Rioja and Catalonia.
- Grenache was first introduced as a California varietal wine by Almadén Vineyards in 1941. _Bouquet & Flavor_: Fruity with an aroma and flavor of black currants, cherry, plum, raspberries and strawberries. Additional hints of fennel, rosemary, thyme, and white pepper.
- _Recommended Cheeses_: Blue Cheeses, Fiore Sardo, and Triple-Crèmes.

Grignolino (gree-nyoh-LEE-noh)

- _Background_: (*Italy*) A high acid, red grape variety grown principally in the Piedmont region, where it produces *DOC* wines. The Grignolino grapevine is indigenous to the Asti area and its presence there can be traced back to 1252. Some Grignolino is also grown in California and Uruguay.
- _Bouquet & Flavor_: Brick-red colored with refined aromas and flavors of dried roses, grapefruit, herbal-floral, clove, white pepper, and spicy nuances. It is light-bodied and fruity.
- _Recommended Cheeses_: Asiago, Bagozzo, Bra, Caciocavallo, Caciotta, Fiore Sardo, Fontina, Gorgonzola, Grana, Parmigiano-Reggiano, Pecorino, Provolone, Robiola Piemonte, Taleggio, and Toma.

Lambrusco (lahm-BROOS-koh)

- _Background_: (*Italy*) A red grape variety indigenous to the Emilia-Romagna region where it is made into a varietal wine, whereas in Apulia, Lombardy, and Trentino-Alto Adige, it is used mostly for blending. The Lambrusco grape can be vinified into a white, rosé, or a red wine, which is typically *frizzante*, although a *spumante* version can be found. There are many strains of the Lambrusco grape variety; among them are di Sorbara (also known as *Sorbarese*), Grasparossa, Maestri, Marani, Montericco, Salamino, and Viadanese.
- _Bouquet & Flavor_: Ruby red to purple in color with an aroma and flavor of wild berries (boysenberry, raspberry, strawberry), cherries, cola, and violets. Slightly tart with a clean, refreshing, lingering tart aftertaste.
- _Recommended Cheeses_: Asiago, Bagozzo, Grana, Parmigiano-Reggiano, and Pecorino.

Madeira (Dry) (mah-DEHR-ah)

- _Background_: (_Portugal_) The largest of three small islands off Portugal in the Atlantic Ocean, some 360 miles from the coast of Morocco, famous for its fortified wines. Madeira is a fortified wine (beginning in 1753) with an alcoholic content of 17 to 20 percent by volume due to the addition of a 96 proof brandy. The five styles of Madeira (driest to sweetest) are Sercial, Verdelho, Rainwater, Boal, and Malmsey.
- _Bouquet & Flavor_: Bouquet and flavor of dried fruit, chocolate, citrus (lemon, orange), coffee, and nuts. Tangy with hints of spices and honey.
- _Recommended Cheeses_: Aostino, Asiago, Blue Cheeses, Caciocavallo, Fontina, Gorgonzola, Parmigiano-Reggiano, Pecorino, Provolone, Scamorza, and Triple-Crèmes.

Malbec (mahl-BEHK)

- _Background_: A thick-skinned, red grape variety, imported into Bordeaux from Cahors at the end of the eighteenth century by M. Malbeck. Malbec is generally blended with Cabernet Sauvignon and Merlot in the red wines of Bordeaux. Malbec is an abundant producer, contributing color and tannin to the wine. It is grown in the Loire Valley as well as in the southwest. Malbec is grown extensively in Argentina (since at least the late 1860s), with plantings in many other countries, including the United States.
- _Bouquet & Flavor_: Deep, dark color, leaning toward purple, with thick staining tears, and a fruity aroma and flavor of berries (blackberry, blueberry, boysenberry, elderberry, mulberry, myrtle, raspberry), cherries, and plums. In addition, black licorice, chocolate, clove, coffee, leather, mint, sage, oak, vanilla, and violets abound.
- _Recommended Cheeses_: Asiago

Marsala (Dry) (mahr-SAH-lah)

- _Background_: (*Italy*) Marsala is both the name of a city in northwest Sicily and the name of a fortified wine made from a blend of grapes indigenous to Sicily.
- Like sherry and port, Marsala is a fortified wine; it bears some resemblance to Madeira in that one or more of its constituents are cooked or heated during the processing.
- The *DOC* law has set production rules for three versions of Marsala. They are: *Marsala Fine, Marsala Superiore,* and *Marsala Vergine* or *Vergine Soleras.*
- _Bouquet & Flavor_: Unique aroma and flavors of burnt raisin, burnt wood, caramel, coffee, figs, nuts (walnuts), raisins, smoke, and toffee with a silky, tangy, apricot taste.
- _Recommended Cheeses_: Aostino, Asiago, Bagozzo, Blue Cheeses, Burrata, Burrini, Caciocavallo, Fiore Sardo, Fontina, Gorgonzola, Grana, Mozzarella, Parmigiano-Reggiano, Pecorino, Provolone, Scamorza, and Triple-Crèmes.

Merlot (mehr-LOH)

- _Background_: A medium-skinned, medium acid, red grape variety acknowledged worldwide as producing some of the finest dry red wines. It is the predominant red grape variety of the Bordeaux region. In the Médoc and Graves district, it is blended in significant amounts with Cabernet Sauvignon and Cabernet Franc; in the districts of Pomerol and Saint-Émilion, it constitutes the predominant grape in the wines. Merlot is also used straight as a varietal in many parts of the world. (*Merlot* is French patois for *Little Blackbird*.)
- Merlot is used extensively to soften and tame the more assertive bitter and tannic Cabernet Sauvignon. Merlot has less tannin than Cabernet Sauvignon and thinner skins, and because they are low in malic acid, the resulting wine is softer. When blended with Cabernet Sauvignon, the resulting wine

develops faster, shortening aging requirements. In 1968, Louis M. Martini Winery of California bottled the first Merlot as a separate varietal.

- *Bouquet & Flavor*: Bright ruby color, producing scented, fruity wines, smelling and tasting very much of bell pepper, berries (blackberry, blueberry, cranberry, raspberry), black cherry, black currants, black olive, black tea, cedar, chocolate, cinnamon, coffee, green olive, herbs, licorice, maraschino cherry, peppermint, plum, spice, tar, tobacco, and violets.
- *Recommended Cheeses*: Asiago, Bagozzo, Bel Paese, Caciocavallo, Fontina, Grana, Parmigiano-Reggiano, Pecorino, Provolone, Robiola Piemonte, Taleggio, and Toma.

Montefalco Sagrantino (mohn-teh-FAHL-koh sah-grahn-TEE-noh)

- *Background*: (*Italy*) A DOCG (1992) red wine produced in the province of Perugia in the communes of Montefalco, Bevagna, Castel Ritaldi, Giano dell'Umbria, and Gualdo Cattaneo, in the Umbria region from Sagrantino grapes. A single-vineyard *secco* and *passito* style is authorized.
- *Bouquet & Flavor*: Dark ruby-red in color tending to garnet, with delicate scents of berries (blackberry, mulberry), fresh and dried plums, cherries, cinnamon, cloves, gingersnaps, nutmeg, and a well-balanced, rich flavor reminiscent of a spice cake, along with a touch of bitterness.
- *Recommended Cheeses*: Gorgonzola, Pecorino, Taleggio

Montepulciano d'Abruzzo (mohn-teh-puhl-CHAH-noh dah-BROOT-zoh)

- *Background*: (*Italy*) A low acid, red grape variety grown principally in Abruzzo; some is also grown in many other regions. It is also a DOC (1968) red wine made in the Abruzzo region, principally from Montepulciano grapes. Montepulciano may be produced in all four of Abruzzo's provinces: Chieti, L'Aquila, Pescara, and Teramo. A *riserva* style is authorized.

- *Bouquet & Flavor*: Rich, deep ruby red color with a bouquet and taste of berries (blackberry, raspberry, strawberry), black licorice, cola, spices (black pepper, cinnamon, nutmeg), cherries, chestnuts, leather, tobacco, roasted almonds, plums, and earthy. Quite fruity with a tart-berry aftertaste.
- *Recommended Cheeses*: Asiago, Bagozzo, Caciotta, Grana, Parmigiano-Reggiano, and Pecorino.

Nebbiolo (nehb-bee-YOH-loh)

- *Background*: (*Italy*) A thin-skinned, late-ripening, red grape variety grown principally in the Piedmont region. Nebbiolo produces wines that are usually rough and tannic when young but with age evolve into wines of extraordinary power, depth, and complexity. When blended with other varieties, the Nebbiolo grape gives the resultant wine body, structure, and substance. The Nebbiolo grape, like Pinot Noir, doesn't provide a lot of color to the wine, which accounts for the sometimes orange or brick color.
- Nebbiolo is not one grape, but a family of grapes whose variations probably arrived through mutation. There are three sub-varieties: Michet, which is the most prized, Lampia, which is widely grown throughout the area, and rose, whose acreage has dwindled over the years. Nebbiolo is used to produce Barolo, Barbaresco, Gattinara, Ghemme, Inferno, Roero Rosso, Sforzato di Valtellina, and many other wines.
- Originally called *Vitis vinifera Pedemontana* (the grapevine of Piedmont), the grape is referred to as *Nubiola, Nebiola, Nibiol,* and *Nebiolium* in documents dating back to 1266. Other documents suggest that Nebbiolo was called *allobrogica* by Pliny the Elder (AD 23–79) in his *Naturalis Historia*. Its present name and spelling, officially sanctioned in 1962, are derived from the

word *nebbia* (fog). Some say that it was given this name because of the persistent fog found in the area of cultivation, while others believe that it alludes to the thick bloom that forms on the grape skins, making them look as if they were surrounded by tiny patches of fog. Nebbiolo is also grown in many countries of the world, especially Argentina. Nebbiolo is known in Italy as *Chiavennasca* and *Spanna*.

- <u>*Bouquet & Flavor*</u>: Deep and dark in color, with characteristic garnet-red highlights that in time mellow into orange. It has an intense bouquet and flavor of fruit—berries (cranberry, raspberry), cherries, jam, mulberry, peaches, prunes, and dried fruit, along with almonds, anise, black pepper, cedar, chocolate, cinnamon, coffee, fennel, licorice, mint, nutmeg, roses, spices, tobacco, violets, and an earthy bouquet of dried roses, eucalyptus, forest leaves, truffles, and withered flowers. It is dry, robust, and full-bodied, yet it nevertheless exhibits a surprising gentle, well-balanced taste.
- <u>*Recommended Cheeses*</u>: Aostino, Asiago, Bagozzo, Bitto, Blue Cheeses, Bra, Burrata, Burrini, Caciocavallo, Fiore Sardo, Fontina, Gorgonzola, Grana, Mozzarella, Parmigiano-Reggiano, Pecorino, Provolone, Robiola Piemonte, Scamorza, Taleggio, and Toma.

Orvieto (ohr-VYEH-toh)
- <u>*Background*</u>: (*Italy*) A *DOC* (1971) white wine made in a city in southwestern Umbria (located in both Umbria and Latium), where wines are produced in the Paglia and Upper Tiber valleys as well as throughout the province of Terni. The Orvieto Classico area is in the heart of this *DOC* zone.
- Orvieto is made principally from Grechetto and Procanico (Trebbiano Toscano) grapes. A *classico, superiore, abboccato, amabile, dolce,* and *vendemmia tardiva* styles are authorized.
- <u>*Bouquet & Flavor*</u>: Straw-colored, with a delicate aroma and flavor of green apple, bitter orange, citrus (lemon, lime), grass,

kiwi, and melon. Light-bodied and dry with a lingering after-taste of almonds.

- _Recommended Cheeses_: Asiago, Bagozzo, Bel Paese, Bitto, Burrata, Burrini, Caciocavallo, Caprini, Fontina, Grana, Mozzarella, Parmigiano-Reggiano, Pecorino, Provolone, Ricotta, Robiola Piemonte, Scamorza, and Taleggio.

Petite Sirah (peh-TEET see-RAH)

- _Background_: (_United States_) A red grape variety grown in California, where it was known under many names and aliases for decades. In September of 1997, DNA testing confirmed that Petite Sirah is in fact a cross between the Rhône Syrah and an obscure French red grape, the Peloursin. In addition, Petite Sirah and the grape Durif are synonymous.
- It was first planted in California in 1884, and in 1964, Concannon Vineyards of Livermore, California, released a 1961 bottling of the grape, the first varietally labeled Petite Sirah to be produced. Also spelled _Petite Syrah_.
- _Bouquet & Flavor_: Inky black color, with a spicy bouquet and flavor of black pepper, blackberry, black cherry, plums, and raisins. Full-bodied and intense, with overtones of herbs, tar, tobacco, and violets, and a powerful aftertaste.
- _Recommended Cheeses_: Asiago, Bagozzo, Bel Paese, Blue Cheeses, Caciotta, Fiore Sardo, Grana, Parmigiano-Reggiano, Pecorino, Provolone, and Triple-Crèmes.

Pinot Bianco (PEE-noh bee-AHN-koh)

- _Background_: (_Italy_) A medium-acid, white grape variety grown in many parts of the world, especially Austria, France, Germany, Hungary, Italy, and the United States. The first plantings of Pinot Bianco in Italy were recorded as early as the 1820s, with experiments carried out by General Emilio di Sambuy. Pinot

Bianco is often used in making sparkling wines. Pinot Bianco is also known as *Pinot Blanc.*

- *Bouquet & Flavor*: Pale, straw hue with brilliant reflections of light green. Aroma and flavor of green apples, apricots, banana, cherries, citrus, coconut, dried fruit, peach, pears, smoke, and spice. Taste is dry and quite crisp with an aftertaste of almonds.
- *Recommended Cheeses*: Bernardo, Blue Cheeses, Burrata, Burrini, Caciocavallo, Fontina, Mozzarella, Ricotta, Scamorza, and Stracchino.

Pinot Grigio (PEE-noh GREE-joh)

- *Background*: (*Italy*) A thin-skinned, medium-acid, white grape variety acknowledged worldwide as producing well-balanced, light-bodied wines. The grape skins range from a bluish gray to a delicate pink color. Pinot Grigio is also known as *Pinot Gris.*
- *Bouquet & Flavor*: Delicate aroma and flavor of apples, citrus (lemon, lime, tangerine), figs, kiwi, melon, nectarine, pears, watercress, and white peach. Its aftertaste is that of almonds and hazelnuts. This dry, light-bodied, crisp wine also has a minerally flinty, almost smoky-floral smell with hints of wet stone and chalk.
- *Recommended Cheeses*: Asiago, Bagozzo, Bel Paese, Bernardo, Burrata, Burrini, Caprini, Fontina, Grana, Montasio, Mozzarella, Parmigiano-Reggiano, Pecorino, Ricotta, Robiola Piemonte, Scamorza, and Stracchino.

Pinot Noir (pee-NOH nwahr)

- *Background*: (*France*) An ancient, thin-skinned, medium acid, red grape variety believed to have originated in France more than 2,000 years ago. Ancient Romans knew this grape as *Helvenacia Minor* and vinified it as early as the first century A.D. Pinot Noir is grown mostly in Burgundy, France, where it produces some of the finest wines in the world, and is also vinified, along with Pinot Meunier and Chardonnay, to produce champagne.

- In Italy, Pinot Noir is known as *Pinot Nero*.
- *Bouquet & Flavor*: Medium to deep ruby-red, with a distinctive aroma and taste of berries (blackberry, cranberry, loganberry, mulberry, raspberry, strawberry), black currant, black pepper, cedar, chocolate, cinnamon, cola, coffee, dried fruits, herbs, jam, mint, plum, pomegranate, prunes, quinine, red currant, spice, tangerine, and wild cherries. Other aromas of barnyard, earth, forest, leather, mushrooms, roses, sandalwood, tomato leaf, truffles, and violets.
- *Recommended Cheeses*: Asiago, Bagozzo, Bel Paese, Blue Cheeses, Caciotta, Caprini, Fontina, Grana, Parmigiano-Reggiano, Pecorino, Provolone, Stracchino, Taleggio, and Triple-Crèmes.

Port
- *Background*: (*Portugal*) A heavy, full-bodied, sweet red or white fortified wine, traditionally served after dinner; it is named for the city of Oporto in northern Portugal. The production and marketing of port are strictly controlled by the *Instituto do Vinho do Porto* (Port Wine Institute), set up in June 1933.
- Although there are more than 80 approved grape varieties in the production of port (white and red), the preferred red grapes are Touriga Nacional, Touriga Franca, Tinta Roriz, Tinto Cão, Tinta Barroca, Trincadeira (Tinta Amarela), Tinta Francisca, Bastardo and Mourisco Tinto.
- *Bouquet & Flavor*: Dark purple-black color with a bouquet and flavor of black pepper, chocolate, cinnamon, cocoa, coffee, dried plums, figs, raisins, toffee, and ripe fruit. Its sweetness is masked by concentrated packed fruit, high extract, fiery-pepper, and dry, mouth-puckering tannins.

- _Recommended Cheeses_: Asiago, Bagozzo, Bel Paese, Blue Cheeses, Gorgonzola, Grana, Parmigiano-Reggiano, Pecorino, and Triple-Crèmes.

Primitivo (pree-mee-TEE-voh)
- _Background_: (_Italy_) A very dark red grape variety grown almost exclusively in southern Italy (Apulia, Basilicata, Campania), often producing wines with residual sugar and high alcohol content. Italian researchers have determined that Primitivo has been cultivated in Puglia for about 150 to 250 years.
- In June 2001, through DNA testing, it was determined that a Croatian grape called Dobrocic and Zinfandel were clearly the parents of Plavac Mali, and that Primitivo and Zinfandel were indeed two clones of Crljenak Kastelanski.
- _Bouquet & Flavor_: Dark, almost black colored with an aroma and flavor of berries (blackberry, blueberry, raspberry), black pepper, cherries, cocoa, dried fruit, licorice, jam, and spices. Dry with an aftertaste of figs, dried plums, and nuts.
- _Recommended Cheeses_: Asiago, Bagozzo, Bitto, Caciocavallo, Fiore Sardo, Gorgonzola, Grana, Pecorino, and Provolone.

Prosecco (proh-SEHK-koh)
- _Background_: (_Italy_): A white wine sparkling made in the regions of Veneto and Friuli-Venezia Giulia. Grapes include Prosecco (Glera), Verdiso, Bianchetta, Perera, Glera Lunga, Chardonnay, Pinot Bianco, Pinot Grigio, and Pinot Noir.
- _Bouquet & Flavor:_ Pale greenish-straw in color. It has a fresh fruity, aroma of acacia blossoms, almonds, anise, green and red apples, apricots, bread dough, citrus (lemon, lime), melon, peaches, pears, and wild flowers. Light, dry, well-balanced, and very clean tasting with a lingering, crispy aftertaste.
- _Recommended Cheeses_: _See_ Champagne and Sparkling Wine (Dry)

Riesling (REEZ-ling)

- _Background_: (_Germany_) A thick-skinned, white grape variety, which is the predominant grape of Germany, producing the best of the distinctive wines of the Rhine and Mosel regions. Riesling also flourishes in Alsace, France; Australia, Austria, and the United States, as well as other parts of the world. Riesling was probably derived from a wild grapevine, _Vitis vinifera silvestris_, still found growing naturally in woods in the upper Rhine of Germany. It first appeared in a written document dated March 13, 1435, which reported it growing near Hochheim in the Rheingau.
- The skins are susceptible to sunburn and infection by _Botrytis cinerea_. In favorable seasons, this tendency can be taken advantage of to produce a late-harvest sweet wine. Riesling produces dry, semidry, sweet, and even sparkling wines.
- _Bouquet & Flavor_: Quite floral, with aromas and flavors of acacia blossoms, allspice, green apple, citrus (lemon, lime, tangerine), clove, curry, dried or fresh flowers, fennel, ginger, grapefruit, guava, honeysuckle, jasmine, kiwi, litchi, mango, mint, orange blossom, papaya, passion fruit, peaches, pear, "_petrol_," pineapple, quince, rhubarb, tarragon, tropical fruits, and Muscat grapes, balanced by good acidity. Other aromas flavors can be flint, minerals, slate, and stone. _Botrytis cinerea_ can add the aroma and flavor of almonds, dried apricot, figs, honey, marzipan, mushrooms, and raisins.
- _Recommended Cheeses_: Asiago, Bagozzo, Bel Paese, Blue Cheeses, Burrata, Burrini, Caprini, Fontina, Grana, Mozzarella, Parmigiano-Reggiano, Pecorino, Provolone, Ricotta, Robiola Piemonte, Scamorza, Taleggio, and Triple-Crèmes.

Rosé (Dry)

- _Background_: A wine made from red grapes that has a light pink color, acquired by short contact with the skins; wine made from a mixture of red and white grapes; or wine made by blending red and white wines. In Italy rosé wine is known as _vino rosato_.

- _Bouquet & Flavor_: Rosé orange tinge and a floral and strawberry, black currants, raspberries, cherry, blackberry bouquet and flavor.
- _Recommended Cheeses_: Burrata, Burrini, Mozzarella, Ricotta, Scamorza, and Triple-Crèmes.

Sangiovese (sahn-joh-VEH-zeh)

- _Background_: (_Italy_) A thin-skinned, high acid, red grape variety grown in most of the 20 regions. Sangiovese is recommended or required as either a blending or a primary grape variety in more than 150 _DOC_ and _DOCG_ wine appellations nationwide. Sangiovese is also grown in many parts of the world, including California and Washington State. Through DNA analysis (2004) it was determined that Sangiovese is a natural cross of Ciliegiolo and Calabrese di Montenuovo. The Sangiovese grape is one of Italy's most noble varieties; originated in Tuscany where it is widely grown. Its name is believed to come from _Sanguis Jovis_, Latin for _Jupiter's Blood_. Sangiovese is also known as _Brunello, Morellino_, and _Prugnolo Gentile_.
- _Bouquet & Flavor_: Aromas and flavors of almonds, anise, bay leaf, berries (blackberry, blueberry, raspberry, strawberry), black tea, cinnamon, clove, hazelnuts, jam, leather, dried plums, red currants, sour cherry, tar, and violets.
- _Recommended Cheeses_: Asiago, Bagozzo, Bel Paese, Blue Cheeses, Burrata, Burrini, Caciocavallo, Caciotta, Calcagno, Fiore Sardo, Fontina, Gorgonzola, Grana, Mozzarella, Parmigiano-Reggiano, Pecorino, Provolone, Robiola Piemonte, Scamorza, Taleggio, and Toma.

Sauvignon Blanc (soh-veen-YOHN blahn)

- _Background_: A high acid, white grape variety grown in most wine-producing countries of the world where it produces mostly dry wines, also semidry and sweet wines. Sauvignon Blanc is very susceptible to *Botrytis cinerea* producing some of the greatest sweet wines in the world.

- In Bordeaux, France, Sauvignon Blanc is blended with Sémillon and Muscadelle to produce either the dry white wines of Graves or the luscious sweet dessert wines of Sauternes. In the Loire Valley, Sauvignon Blanc is used in making Pouilly Fumé, Sancerre, Ménétou-Salon, Reuilly, and Quincy, which are often described as being *flinty*.

- In 1997, Carole Meredith, a professor of enology and viticulture at the University of California at Davis, revealed Cabernet Sauvignon's parentage through DNA testing. She stated that it is "150 trillion times" more likely that Cabernet Franc and Sauvignon Blanc– rather than any other varieties– were responsible for the cross-pollination leading to Cabernet Sauvignon's appearance in the late seventeenth century.

- In California, it is speculated that Sauvignon Blanc was first grown around the 1850s, although it made its first appearance in 1878 in the Livermore Valley and wasn't bottled as a separate varietal until Wente Vineyards 1932 vintage (released in 1934). In the United States (also other countries), Sauvignon Blanc is also known as and can legally be labeled as *Fumé Blanc*.

- <u>*Bouquet & Flavor*</u>: Apple, apricot, asparagus, bay leaf, bell pepper, black pepper, celery, citrus (grapefruit, pink grapefruit, lemon, lime), dill, fennel, figs (green), flint, gooseberry, grass, green bean, green fig, green olive, green pea, guava, hawthorn, hay, honeysuckle, jalapeño, jasmine, kiwi, lemongrass, melon (cantaloupe, honeydew), mineral, mint, nectarine, passion fruit, pea pod, peach, pear (Anjou), pineapple, radish, sage, shale, straw, sugar snap peas, tangerine, tarragon, tomato leaf, and new-mown grass that can sometimes be quite herbaceous. If barrel-fermented or aged in wood, aromas and flavors of nuts, smoke, and toast.

- *Recommended Cheeses*: Asiago, Bagozzo, Bel Paese, Blue Cheeses, Burrata, Burrini, Caciotta, Caprini, Fiore Sardo, Fontina, Gorgonzola, Grana, Mozzarella, Parmigiano-Reggiano, Pecorino, Provolone, Ricotta, Robiola Piemonte, Scamorza, Taleggio, and Triple-Crèmes.

Scotch Whisky

- *Background*: (*Scotland*) A distinctive product of Scotland made in compliance with the 1909 laws of Great Britain as well as the Scotch Whisky Act of 2009. The whisky can legally be called Scotch if it is distilled and matured in Scotland and made from water and cereal grains, and fermented by the addition of yeast. Scotch is distilled twice (or more). Its distinctive smoky taste comes from the peat fires over which the barley malt is dried. However, there is no regulation that requires the use of peat to dry the barley. Its primary base grain is barley (distilled by pot stills for heavy-bodied whisky) or corn (distilled by continuous still for lighter-bodied whisky). There are two basic types of Scotch—Blended and Single Malt. Most Scotch whisky is a blend of malt and grain whiskies.
- *Recommended Cheeses*: Bagozzo and Caciocavallo

Semisweet to Sweet Wines

- *Recommended Cheeses*: Aostino, Asiago, Bagozzo, Blue Cheeses, Burrata, Burrini, Caciocavallo, Fiore Sardo, Gorgonzola, Grana, Mozzarella, Parmigiano-Reggiano, Pecorino, Provolone, Scamorza, and Triple-Crèmes.

Sherry (Dry)

- *Background*: (*Spain*) A fortified and blended nonvintage wine made via the *solera system* and containing 17 to 22 percent alcohol. Sherry is traditionally produced in Spain, although certain other countries produce a similar product they call sherry.

- Sherry originated in southwest Andalusia in the Jerez region. The town of Jerez was founded by the Phoenicians in 1100 B.C.; they brought their sailing ships to an inland city near the Bay of Cádiz on the Atlantic coast and named it *Xera*. After the Roman conquest, Xera was Latinized to *Ceret*, which the Moors pronounced as *Scherris*. This was subsequently Hispanicized to *Jerez* and anglicized, in reference to the beverage, into *sherry*. Sherry is made principally from Palomino Fino grapes, with small amounts of Moscatel and Pedro Ximénez grapes.
- *Bouquet & Flavor*: Very dry, light, and pale in color, with a distinctive mild nutty-tangy taste.
- *Recommended Cheeses*: Asiago, Bagozzo, Bernardo, Blue Cheeses, Burrata, Burrini, Caciocavallo, Fontina, Gorgonzola, Mozzarella, Parmigiano-Reggiano, Pecorino, Provolone, Scamorza, and Triple-Crèmes.

Sherry (Semisweet)

- *Background*: (*Spain*) A fortified and blended nonvintage wine made via the *solera system* and containing 17 to 22 percent alcohol. Sherry is traditionally produced in Spain, although certain other countries produce a similar product they call sherry.
- Sherry originated in southwest Andalusia in the Jerez region. The town of Jerez was founded by the Phoenicians in 1100 B.C.; they brought their sailing ships to an inland city near the Bay of Cádiz on the Atlantic coast and named it *Xera*. After the Roman conquest, Xera was Latinized to *Ceret*, which the Moors pronounced as *Scherris*. This was subsequently Hispanicized to *Jerez* and anglicized, in reference to the beverage, into *sherry*. Sherry is made principally from Palomino Fino grapes, with small amounts of Moscatel and Pedro Ximénez grapes.

- *Bouquet & Flavor*: Rich, deep amber to a golden brown in color, and usually display an exquisite bouquet. They are very sweet and "creamy" to the taste.
- *Recommended Cheeses*: Bel Paese and Taleggio.

Soave (SWAH-veh)

- *Background*: (*Italy*) A DOC (1968) white wine produced in the communes of Soave, Monteforte d'Alpone, San Martino, and others in the province of Verona, in the Veneto region. Soave is named after a medieval walled town, which stands, dominated by its imposing castle, on the lower slopes of an intensely cultivated vineyard area in the hills east of Verona. It is said that the town's name derives from *Svevi* or *Suavi*, after the Swabians who invaded Italy in the sixth century. The first written citation of Soave as a beverage dates back to the year 568. The first single-vineyard Soave was produced in 1971 by Leonildo Pieropan with his Soave *Calvarino*. The *consorzio* of Soave features a Roman arena at Verona on its neck label.
- Soave is made principally from Garganega grapes with some Trebbiano di Soave and Chardonnay permitted. A *classico* and *spumante* styles are authorized.
- *Bouquet & Flavor*: Straw yellow, tending at times to the greenish. A very fruity aroma and taste of apple, honeydew melon, and pear. It is dry, light-bodied, and balanced, with a slightly bitter-almond aftertaste.
- *Recommended Cheeses*: Bel Paese, Burrata, Burrini, Caciotta, Caprini, Fontina, Mozzarella, Provolone, Ricotta, Robiola Piemonte, Scamorza, Stracchino, and Taleggio.

Syrah (see-RAH)

- *Background*: (*France*) A thick-skinned, red grape variety grown principally in the Rhône Valley of southern France. Syrah is the major grape in the blend of such great wines as Hermitage, Cornas, and Côte Rôtie, to name just a few. It also grown prolifically in Australia, where it is known as *Shiraz*, while some is also grown in California, where for years it was mistakenly identified as *Petite Sirah* or *Petite Syrah*. In 2001, the heritage of the grape was determined through DNA testing. It was determined that Syrah is a cross between Mondeuse Blanche and Dureza, an obscure red grape variety from France's northern Ardèche area, west of the Rhône River.

- In Australia, Syrah is often incorrectly referred to as *Hermitage*, the name of a great red-wine-producing village in the Rhône Valley as well as the local name for the Cinsaut grape variety in South Africa.

- *Bouquet & Flavor*: Dark colored, full-bodied, and long-lived wines, with fruit aromas and flavors of berries (blackberry, blueberry, cranberry, elderberry, mulberry, raspberry, strawberry); black cherry, black currant, plum, pomegranate, and prune. Other aromas and flavors imparted include allspice, barnyard, black pepper, black tea, cedar, chocolate, cinnamon, cloves, coconut, coffee, green pepper, ground ginger, leather, licorice, pepper, peppermint, roasted nuts, rosemary, sage, smoked bacon, spices, tobacco, truffles, violets, and wild mushrooms.

- *Recommended Cheeses*: Blue Cheeses and Triple-Crèmes.

Trebbiano (trehb-bee-AH-noh)

- *Background*: (*Italy*) A white grape variety grown principally throughout Italy, although it is also grown in lesser quantities in France and California. Supposedly, the grape takes its name from the Trebbia River in the Emilia-Romagna region. The grape is believed to have originated in Tuscany in the thirteenth century and exported to France around the time of the Pope's transfer to Avignon from Rome. There was once even a black

Trebbiano grape, no longer in existence, around the mid-1300s. In the Cognac region of France, the grape is known as *St-Emilion* and *Ugni Blanc* (a name also used in California). The Trebbiano grape often takes its full name from the district, town, or region where it is cultivated.

- *Bouquet & Flavor*: Pale straw-colored with a fresh, fruity aroma and flavor of apples, citrus (grapefruit, lemon), melons, and pears, and a bitter almond aftertaste.
- *Recommended Cheeses*: Asiago, Bagozzo, Caciotta, Grana, Parmigiano-Reggiano, and Pecorino.

Valpolicella (vahl-poh-lee-CHEHL-lah)

- *Background*: (*Italy*) A *DOC* (1968) red wine produced in the territories of the communes of Fumane, Negrar, Marano, Sant'Ambrogio di Valpolicella, and San Pietro in Cairano, in the province of Verona, in the Veneto region. There is one official subzone, Valpantena, to the east of the Classico zone. The best wines are likely to come from the inner *classico* zone and are so labeled. Valpolicella is made principally from Corvina Veronese, Corvinone, and Rondinella grapes, with lesser amounts of Molinara, Dindarella, Oseleta, Sangiovese, Cabernet Franc, Cabernet Sauvignon, Merlot, and Teroldego. The consorzio of Valpolicella features the Roman arena at Verona on its neck label. A *classico* and *superiore* styles are authorized.
- *Bouquet & Flavor*: Bright ruby-red in color, tending to garnet with aging, with an appealing bouquet and flavor of bitter almonds, black cherries, dried cherries, dried flowers, mint, nuts, plums, raisins, raspberries, spices, tarragon, tea, tobacco, violets, and wild mushrooms. The wine is dry, velvety, medium-bodied, bitterish, and balanced, with good acidity, tannin, and a warming, lingering aftertaste.
- *Recommended Cheeses*: Asiago, Bagozzo, Bel Paese, Burrata, Burrini, Caciocavallo, Fiore Sardo, Fontina, Gorgonzola,

Grana, Mozzarella, Parmigiano-Reggiano, Pecorino, Provolone, Scamorza, Taleggio, and Toma.

Verdicchio (vehr-DEE-kee-oh)

- _Background_: (_Italy_) A high acid, white grape variety grown principally in the Marches region, although some is grown in Abruzzo, Latium, Lombardy, and Umbria. The name Verdicchio is said to be derived from the greenish (_verde_) highlights in the wine.
- Verdicchio is an indigenous grapevine, which, according to legend, was used to make the wine consumed by the Visigoths in 410 A.D. as they sacked Rome. The first written reference of the Verdicchio grape was in 1569, by a register called _Costanzo Felici_. The first production of a sparkling wine dates back to 1857. Verdicchio is occasionally bottled in the traditional amphora-shaped bottles that were used to bring wine from Greece to the Italian peninsula in ancient times. It is one of the oldest wine bottle shapes in the world, predating the Bordeaux bottle. Verdicchio is made in dry, semidry, sparkling, and even _passito_ versions.
- _Bouquet & Flavor_: Straw colored with green reflections. An intensely perfumed aroma and taste of apples, apricots, citrus (grapefruit, lime, orange), herbs, honeysuckle, minerals, peach, and pears. Very clean and crisp tasting with a bitter-almond (pignoli) aftertaste.
- _Recommended Cheeses_: Asiago, Bagozzo, Bel Paese, Burrata, Burrini, Caciocavallo, Fontina, Grana, Mozzarella, Parmigiano-Reggiano, Pecorino, Ricotta, Scamorza, and Stracchino.

Vermouth (Dry)

- _Background_: According to the United States Bureau of Alcohol, Tobacco, and Firearms, vermouth is a type of apéritif wine that is made from grape juice and has the taste, aroma, and characteristics generally attributed to vermouth. The ATTTB regulations also state that apéritif wines fulfilling the characteristics of vermouth shall be so designated. Vermouth, although fortified (containing between 15 to 21 percent alcohol), is often referred to as an *aromatic* or *aromatized* wine, meaning a wine that has been altered by the infusion of *Artemisia absinthium* (any of a number of related aromatic plants) or bitter herbs. Some of the ingredients used (there are more than 100) are allspice, angelica, angostura, anise, benzoin, bitter almond, bitter orange, celery, chamomile, cinnamon, clove, coca, coriander, elder, fennel, gentian, ginger, hop, marjoram, mace, myrtle, nutmeg, peach, quinine (cinchona bark), rhubarb, rosemary, saffron, sage, sandalwood, savory (summer), thyme, vanilla, and woodruff, which is used to make May wine.

- The red vermouths, most notably those from Italy and France, are always sweet and white vermouths, also mainly from Italy and France, can be dry, semidry, or sweet.
- *Bouquet & Flavor*: Light, pale-yellow in color with a full perfumed bouquet of spices, hints of orange peel and herbs, with none dominating. Dry, with a lemon fresh taste, a full-flavor of fruit, herbs; not high in acidity. Long, pleasing aftertaste.
- *Recommended Cheeses*: Burrata, Burrini, Mozzarella, and Triple-Crèmes.

Vermouth (Sweet)

- *Background*: According to the United States Bureau of Alcohol, Tobacco, and Firearms, vermouth is a type of apéritif wine that is made from grape juice and has the taste, aroma, and characteristics generally attributed to vermouth. The ATTTB regulations also state that apéritif wines fulfilling the characteristics of vermouth shall be so designated. Vermouth, although fortified (containing between 15 to 21 percent alcohol), is often referred to as an *aromatic* or *aromatized* wine, meaning a wine that has been altered by the infusion of *Artemisia absinthium* (any of a number of related aromatic plants) or bitter herbs. Some of the ingredients used (there are more than 100) are allspice, angelica, angostura, anise, benzoin, bitter almond, bitter orange, celery, chamomile, cinnamon, clove, coca, coriander, elder, fennel, gentian, ginger, hop, marjoram, mace, myrtle, nutmeg, peach, quinine (cinchona bark), rhubarb, rosemary, saffron, sage, sandalwood, savory (summer), thyme, vanilla, and woodruff, which is used to make May wine.

- The red vermouths, most notably those from Italy and France, are always sweet and white vermouths, also mainly from Italy and France, can be dry, semidry, or sweet.
- *Bouquet & Flavor*: Red-brown color with a full bouquet of spices…cinnamon, ginger, nutmeg, cloves; reminiscent of a "spice cake." Heavy and full, smooth spicy, bitter-sweet taste, leaning towards bitter; well-balanced and definitely not cloying; not as herbaceous as the dry. Long, lingering, pleasing aftertaste.
- *Recommended Cheeses*: Aostino, Asiago, Bagozzo, Blue Cheeses, Caciocavallo, Fiore Sardo, Gorgonzola, Grana, Mozzarella, Parmigiano-Reggiano, Pecorino, Provolone, and Scamorza.

Vin Santo (VEEN SAHN-toh)

- *Background*: (*Italy*) This unfortified dessert wine is produced in several regions of Italy, each claiming that theirs is the true area of origin. Vin Santo Toscano is made from the ripest Malvasia del Chianti grapes (although Trebbiano Toscano, Grechetto, or even red grapes can be utilized), which are tied together and either hung from the beams of a well-ventilated room or dried on straw mats. This process results in the evaporation of a high percentage of the grapes' water content, at the same time increasing the percentage of sugar. The higher the sugar content of the grape, the higher the resulting alcoholic content and the richer the final product. For a sweet Vin Santo, bunches are left to raisin for about two-and-one-half months; for a Vin Santo that is semidry to dry, they are left about two months.

- The grapes are crushed during the winter and the *must* placed in oak barrels with a capacity of approximately 59 gallons for about two years, followed by three years in smaller chestnut or oak barrels called *caratelli*, which have a capacity of approximately 13 gallons. The same barrels are used repeatedly and a small amount of the previous Vin Santo (*madre*) is left inside to blend with the new *must* (similar to sherry solera production). The barrels are filled to three-quarters capacity, closed with a cork or wooden bung, and placed in the winery's attic or a heated room called a *Vinsanteria*, where the wine is left to ferment slowly. Each winter, fermentation is interrupted by the cold, but it starts again in the spring. During fermentation, carbon dioxide accumulates and creates high pressure that slows down the process. For this reason, the barrels are stored directly under the roof of the winery, where the summer heat causes the wood of the top part of the barrel not in contact with the wine to contract, allowing air to enter and oxidation to occur. This gives Vin Santo its characteristic golden-yellow to amber color and contributes to the complexity of its aroma. Another characteristic of this special aging process is the development of a somewhat cooked or *maderized* taste in the wine.

- This famous Tuscan dessert wine was called *Vino Pretto* until 1349, when the name changed to Vin Santo. The origin of this unusual name has not been firmly established. Some sources claim the wine is called *saintly* because it is used during Holy Mass or because the grapes are crushed during Holy Week. Others claim that during the Ecumenical Council in Florence called by Pope Eugenius VI in 1349, Cardinal Bessarione of Nicaea, patriarch of the Greek Orthodox church, upon being served a glass of Vin Pretto, exclaimed, "This is the Wine of Xantos," referring to a wine from his homeland. His colleagues understood him to be calling the wine *Santo* and the name stuck. Whichever story one believes, one thing is for sure: the name Vin Santo literally means *holy wine* or *wine of the Saints*. Vin Santo is occasionally spelled *vino santo*.

- *Bouquet & Flavor*: An intensely golden-yellow to amber color with a distinctive and unmistakable nutty bouquet, with overtones of cream, apricots, and various types of nuts (hazelnut, pecan, or walnut). Its taste is extremely rich, with a somewhat nutty-creamy, tangy taste reminiscent of dried apricots, which is similar to that of an amontillado sherry, Boal Madeira, dry Marsala, or tawny port. The dry version is an excellent apéritif, served chilled from the refrigerator, while the sweeter Vin Santo is best enjoyed at room temperature after dinner.
- *Recommended Cheeses*: Gorgonzola, Parmigiano-Reggiano, Pecorino, Provolone, and Taleggio.

Zinfandel (Red) (ZIN-fahn-dehl)

- *Background*: (*United States*) A red grape variety with a mysterious past has been grown throughout California for more than 150 years. For decades, it was believed that Agoston Haraszthy, a Hungarian count, often referred to as the "Father of American Viticulture," was responsible for bringing the elusive Zinfandel grape from Hungary to the United States in the mid-1860s. However, our search begins some 30 years earlier with William Robert Prince (1795–1869) a nurseryman who operated the elegantly named Linnaean Botanical Gardens in Flushing, Queens, New York. In his time, he had the largest collection of *Vitis vinifera* grape varieties in America. He experimented extensively with many varieties of grapes and offered Zinfandel, a red grape variety of unknown origin, in his 1830 catalog, listed as *Black St. Peters*.
- In December 2001, it was confirmed through DNA testing that Zinfandel and an indigenous Croatian grape called Crljenak

Kastelanski are one and the same. In June 2001, it was also determined that a Croatian grape called Dobrocic and Zinfandel were clearly the parents of Plavac Mali, and that Primitivo and Zinfandel were indeed two clones of Crljenak Kastelanski. It is speculated that the Crljenak could have been brought to Croatia from Albania or Greece. A small amount of Zinfandel is also grown in Australia, Israel, Italy, New Zealand, and South Africa.

- California's first White Zinfandel was made by George West, from Massachusetts, at the El Pinal Winery, near Stockton, California, in 1869; the first varietally labeled Zinfandel was produced in 1944 by the Parducci Winery; and the first rosé Zinfandel was introduced in 1955 by Pedroncelli Winery. Sutter Home was really the winery that defined and popularized the White Zinfandel category and craze in the early 1970s. The first blush of rosé made in the United States was produced by Almadén Vineyards in the early 1940s, with their Grenache Rosé, a sweetish pink wine. The term *Blush* wine was first used in 1976, by Charlie Kreck, owner of the Mill Creek Winery, later trademarked in 1978.

- *Bouquet & Flavor*: Deep, dark purple-black color, with a full aroma and flavor of anise, baked apples, berries (blackberry, black raspberry, blueberry, boysenberry, loganberry), cherry, chocolate, jam, mint, mocha, nuts, pomegranate, dried plums, raisins, spices (cardamom, cinnamon, clove, nutmeg), vanilla, and toasted oak. Also present are black and white pepper, cedar, coffee, eucalyptus, herbs, leather, minerals, roses, soy, and tobacco.

- *Recommended Cheeses*: Asiago, Bagozzo, Bel Paese, Blue Cheeses, Burrata, Burrini, Caciocavallo, Caciotta, Caprini, Fiore Sardo, Fontina, Gorgonzola, Grana, Mozzarella, Parmigiano-Reggiano, Pecorino, Provolone, Scamorza, Taleggio, and Triple-Crèmes.

Zinfandel (White)

- *Bouquet & Flavor*: A light pink-colored wine with a zesty aroma and flavor of cherry and strawberry, and a crisp, off-dry taste.
- *Recommended Cheeses*: Burrata, Burrini, Fontina, Mozzarella, and Scamorza.

Wine (And Other Beverages) & Cheese Recommendations

Name of Beverage/ Color/ Dry—Semisweet/ Sweet	Name of Cheese
Aglianico (Red) Dry	Asiago, Bagozzo, Blue Cheeses, Caciocavallo, Fiore Sardo, Gorgonzola, Grana, Parmigiano-Reggiano, Pecorino, Provolone
Amarone della Valpolicella (Red) Dry	Aostino, Asiago, Bagozzo, Bitto, Fiore Sardo, Gorgonzola, Grana, Parmigiano-Reggiano, Pecorino, Provolone, Taleggio
Barbera (Red) Dry	Asiago, Bagozzo, Bel Paese, Blue Cheeses, Bra, Caciocavallo, Fiore Sardo, Fontina, Gorgonzola, Grana, Parmigiano-Reggiano, Pecorino, Provolone, Ricotta, Toma
Bardolino (Red) Dry	Asiago, Bagozzo, Bel Paese, Blue Cheeses, Burrata, Burrini, Caciocavallo, Fontina, Grana, Mozzarella, Parmigiano-Reggiano, Pecorino, Provolone, Ricotta, Robiola Piemonte, Scamorza, Taleggio, Toma
Bourbon and Tennessee Whiskey (Brown) Dry	Asiago, Bagozzo, Grana, Parmigiano-Reggiano, Pecorino
Brandy (Grapes)	Blue Cheeses, Gorgonzola, Triple Crèmes
Cabernet Sauvignon (Red) Dry	Asiago, Bagozzo, Blue Cheeses, Burrata, Burrini, Caciocavallo, Caciotta, Fiore Sardo, Fontina, Gorgonzola, Grana, Mozzarella, Parmigiano-Reggiano, Pecorino, Pressato, Provolone, Scamorza, Taleggio, Triple-Crèmes
Carmenère (Red) Dry	Blue Cheeses, Fontina

Champagne and Sparkling Wine (Dry)	Asiago, Bagozzo, Blue Cheeses, Fontina, Grana, Parmigiano-Reggiano, Pecorino, Pressato, Triple-Crèmes
Champagne and Sparkling Wine (Semisweet to Sweet)	Aostino, Gorgonzola, Ricotta
Chardonnay (White) Dry	Asiago, Bagozzo, Bel Paese, Blue Cheeses, Burrata, Burrini, Caciocavallo, Fontina, Grana, Mozzarella, Parmigiano-Reggiano, Pecorino, Provolone, Ricotta, Scamorza, Taleggio, Triple-Crèmes
Chenin Blanc (White) Dry to sweet—sparkling	Aostino, Bel Paese, Burrata, Burrini, Mozzarella, Ricotta, Scamorza, Taleggio, Triple-Crèmes
Cortese (White) Dry	Asiago, Bagozzo, Bitto, Blue Cheeses, Caciocavallo, Fontina, Grana, Parmigiano-Reggiano, Pecorino, Robiola Piemonte, Taleggio, Triple-Crèmes
Dolcetto (Red) Dry	Asiago, Bagozzo, Blue Cheeses, Burrata, Burrini, Fontina, Gorgonzola, Grana, Montasio, Mozzarella, Parmigiano-Reggiano, Pecorino, Provolone, Ricotta, Robiola Piemonte, Scamorza, Taleggio, Toma
Fiano (White) Dry	Asiago, Bagozzo, Fiore Sardo, Grana, Parmigiano-Reggiano, Pecorino
Frascati (White) Dry—Semisweet	Bel Paese, Burrata, Burrini, Caprini, Mozzarella, Ricotta, Scamorza
Friulano (White) Dry	Asiago, Bagozzo, Bernardo, Fontina, Gorgonzola, Grana, Parmigiano-Reggiano, Pecorino, Provolone
Gamay (Red) Dry	Bel Paese, Blue Cheeses, Burrata, Burrini, Fontina, Mozzarella, Scamorza, Taleggio, Triple-Crèmes
Gewürztraminer (White) Dry—sweet	Asiago, Bagozzo, Bernardo, Blue Cheeses, Fontina, Gorgonzola, Grana, Mozzarella, Parmigiano-Reggiano, Pecorino, Provolone, Ricotta, Scamorza, Triple-Crèmes
Grappa (Clear—Brown) Dry	Gorgonzola
Greco (White) Dry	Caciocavallo, Calcagno, Fiore Sardo, Provolone
Grenache (Red) Dry	Blue Cheeses, Fiore Sardo, Triple-Crèmes
Grignolino (Red) Dry	Asiago, Bagozzo, Bra, Caciocavallo, Caciotta, Fiore Sardo, Fontina, Gorgonzola, Grana, Parmigiano-Reggiano, Pecorino, Provolone, Robiola Piemonte, Taleggio, Toma
Lambrusco (Red) Dry–Semisweet	Asiago, Bagozzo, Grana, Parmigiano-Reggiano, Pecorino

Madeira (Amber) Dry	Aostino, Asiago, Blue Cheeses, Caciocavallo, Fontina, Gorgonzola, Parmigiano-Reggiano, Pecorino, Provolone, Scamorza, Triple-Crèmes
Malbec (Red) Dry	Asiago
Marsala (Dry)	Aostino, Asiago, Bagozzo, Blue Cheeses, Burrata, Burrini, Caciocavallo, Fiore Sardo, Fontina, Gorgonzola, Grana, Mozzarella, Parmigiano-Reggiano, Pecorino, Provolone, Scamorza, Triple-Crèmes
Merlot (Red) Dry	Asiago, Bagozzo, Bel Paese, Caciocavallo, Fontina, Grana, Parmigiano-Reggiano, Pecorino, Provolone, Robiola Piemonte, Taleggio, Toma
Montefalco Sagrantino (Red) Dry	Gorgonzola, Pecorino, Taleggio
Montepulciano d'Abruzzo (Red) Dry	Asiago, Bagozzo, Caciotta, Grana, Parmigiano-Reggiano, Pecorino
Nebbiolo (Red) Dry	Aostino, Asiago, Bagozzo, Bitto, Blue Cheeses, Bra, Burrata, Burrini, Caciocavallo, Fiore Sardo, Fontina, Gorgonzola, Grana, Mozzarella, Parmigiano-Reggiano, Pecorino, Provolone, Robiola Piemonte, Scamorza, Taleggio, Toma
Orvieto (White) Dry— Semisweet	Asiago, Bagozzo, Bel Paese, Bitto, Burrata, Burrini, Caciocavallo, Caprini, Fontina, Grana, Mozzarella, Parmigiano-Reggiano, Pecorino, Provolone, Ricotta, Robiola Piemonte, Scamorza, Taleggio
Petite Sirah (Red) Dry	Asiago, Bagozzo, Bel Paese, Blue Cheeses, Caciotta, Fiore Sardo, Grana, Parmigiano-Reggiano, Pecorino, Provolone, Triple-Crèmes
Pinot Bianco (White) Dry	Bernardo, Blue Cheeses, Burrata, Burrini, Caciocavallo, Fontina, Mozzarella, Ricotta, Scamorza
Pinot Grigio (White) Dry	Asiago, Bagozzo, Bel Paese, Bernardo, Burrata, Burrini, Caprini, Fontina, Grana, Montasio, Mozzarella, Parmigiano-Reggiano, Pecorino, Ricotta, Robiola Piemonte, Scamorza
Pinot Noir (Red) Dry	Asiago, Bagozzo, Bel Paese, Blue Cheeses, Caciotta, Caprini, Fontina, Grana, Parmigiano-Reggiano, Pecorino, Provolone, Taleggio, Triple-Crèmes
Port (White–Red) Semisweet	Asiago, Bagozzo, Bel Paese, Blue Cheeses, Gorgonzola, Grana, Parmigiano-Reggiano, Pecorino, Triple-Crèmes

Primitivo (Red) Dry	Asiago, Bagozzo, Bitto, Caciocavallo, Fiore Sardo, Gorgonzola, Grana, Pecorino, Provolone
Riesling (White) Dry—Sweet	Asiago, Bagozzo, Bel Paese, Blue Cheeses, Burrata, Burrini, Caprini, Fontina, Grana, Mozzarella, Parmigiano-Reggiano, Pecorino, Provolone, Ricotta, Robiola Piemonte, Scamorza, Taleggio, Triple-Crèmes
Rosé (Dry)	Burrata, Burrini, Mozzarella, Ricotta, Scamorza, Triple-Crèmes
Sangiovese (Red) Dry	Asiago, Bagozzo, Bel Paese, Blue Cheeses, Burrata, Burrini, Caciocavallo, Caciotta, Calcagno, Fiore Sardo, Fontina, Gorgonzola, Grana, Mozzarella, Parmigiano-Reggiano, Pecorino, Provolone, Robiola Piemonte, Scamorza, Taleggio, Toma
Sauvignon Blanc (White) Dry—Semisweet	Asiago, Bagozzo, Bel Paese, Blue Cheeses, Burrata, Burrini, Caciotta, Caprini, Fiore Sardo, Fontina, Gorgonzola, Grana, Montasio, Mozzarella, Parmigiano-Reggiano, Pecorino, Provolone, Ricotta, Robiola Piemonte, Scamorza, Taleggio, Triple-Crèmes
Scotch Whisky (Amber) Dry	Bagozzo, Caciocavallo
Semisweet to Sweet Wines	Aostino, Asiago, Bagozzo, Blue Cheeses, Burrata, Burrini, Caciocavallo, Fiore Sardo, Gorgonzola, Grana, Mozzarella, Parmigiano-Reggiano, Pecorino, Provolone, Scamorza, Triple-Crèmes
Sherry (Amber) Dry	Asiago, Bagozzo, Bernardo, Blue Cheeses, Burrata, Burrini, Caciocavallo, Fontina, Gorgonzola, Mozzarella, Parmigiano-Reggiano, Pecorino, Provolone, Scamorza, Triple-Crèmes
Sherry (Amber) Semisweet	Bel Paese, Taleggio
Soave (White) Dry	Bel Paese, Burrata, Burrini, Caciotta, Caprini, Fontina, Mozzarella, Provolone, Ricotta, Robiola Piemonte, Scamorza, Taleggio
Syrah (Red) Dry	Blue Cheeses, Triple-Crèmes
Tempranillo (Red) Dry	Blue Cheeses
Trebbiano d'Abruzzo (White) Dry	Asiago, Bagozzo, Caciotta, Grana, Parmigiano-Reggiano, Pecorino
Valpolicella (Red) Dry	Asiago, Bagozzo, Bel Paese, Burrata, Burrini, Caciocavallo, Fiore Sardo, Fontina, Gorgonzola, Grana, Mozzarella, Parmigiano-Reggiano, Pecorino, Provolone, Scamorza, Taleggio, Toma

Verdicchio (White) Dry	Asiago, Bagozzo, Bel Paese, Burrata, Burrini, Caciocavallo, Fontina, Grana, Mozzarella, Parmigiano-Reggiano, Pecorino, Ricotta, Scamorza
Vermouth (White) Dry	Burrata, Burrini, Mozzarella, Triple-Crèmes
Vermouth (White or Red) Sweet	Aostino, Asiago, Bagozzo, Blue Cheeses, Caciocavallo, Fiore Sardo, Gorgonzola, Grana, Mozzarella, Parmigiano-Reggiano, Pecorino, Provolone, Scamorza
Vin Santo (Amber) Semi-sweet	Gorgonzola, Parmigiano-Reggiano, Pecorino, Provolone, Taleggio
Zinfandel (Red) Dry	Asiago, Bagozzo, Bel Paese, Blue Cheeses, Burrata, Burrini, Caciocavallo, Caciotta, Caprini, Fiore Sardo, Fontina, Gorgonzola, Grana, Mozzarella, Parmigiano-Reggiano, Pecorino, Provolone, Scamorza, Taleggio, Triple-Crèmes
Zinfandel (White) Semi-sweet	Burrata, Burrini, Fontina, Mozzarella, Scamorza

Regions Where Cheese is Made

Abruzzo
Scamorza
Scanno

Apulia
Burrata
Burrini
Caciocavallo Silano
Canestrato Pugliese
Foggiano
Gravina
Incanestrato
Mozzarella di Bufala Campana
Pecorino Canestrato
Ricotta di Bufala Campana
Ricotta Salata
Scamorza

Basilicata
Burrata
Burrini
Caciocavallo Silano
Casiddi
Gravina
Pecorino di Filiano

Calabria
Abbespata
Burrata
Burrini
Caciocavallo Silano
Canestrato
Crotonese
Incanestrato
Pecorino Canestrato
Scamorza

Campania
Bocconcini
Burrini
Caciocavallo Silano
Mozzarella
Mozzarella di Bufala Campana
Provolone del Monaco
Ricotta di Bufala Campana
Ricotta Salata
Scamorza

Emilia-Romagna
Formaggio di Fossa di Sogliano
Grana Padano
Parmigiano-Reggiano
Provolone Valpadana
Squacquerone di Romagna

Friuli-Venezia Giulia
Montasio

Latium
Caciotta Romano
Caciotte del Lazio
Caprino Romano
Mozzarella di Bufala Campana
Pecorino di Picinisco
Pecorino Romano
Ricotta di Bufala Campana
Ricotta Romana
Ricotta Salata
Vacchino Romano

Liguria
Chiavara
Prescinseua

Lombardy
Bagozzo
Bel Paese
Bernardo
Bitto
Branzi
Caciotta di Lodi
Caprini di Montevecchia
Certosa
Crescenza
Formaggella del Luinese
Formai de Mut dell'Alta Valle Brembana
Gorgonzola
Gorgonzola Bianco
Grana Padano
Granone Lodigiano
Italico
Mascarpone
Nostrano Valtrompia
Paglia
Provolone Lombardo
Provolone Valpadana
Quartirolo Lombardo
Salva Cremasco
Silter
Stracchino
Taleggio
Toma
Valtellina Casera

Marches
Caciotta d'Urbino
Caciotte delle Marche
Casciotta d'Urbino
Formaggio di Fossa di Sogliano
Pecorino di San Leo

Molise
Caciocavallo Silano
Mozzarella di Bufala Campana
Ricotta di Bufala Campana
Scamorza

Piedmont
Acceglio
Blu del Moncenisio
Bra
Bross
Brucialepre
Caprino Piemontese
Castagneto
Casteljosina
Castelmagno
Cevrin di Coazze
Crescenza
Fagottini
Gorgonzola
Gorgonzola Bianco
Grana Padano

Grasso d'Alpe
Montebore
Murazzano
Paglia
Raschera
Ricotta Piemontese
Robiola delle Langhe
Robiola di Bossolasco
Robiola di Cocconato
Robiola di Roccaverano
Robiola Piemonte
Taleggio
Toma
Toma Piemontese
Tometta
Tomini

Sardinia
Brigante
Calcagno
Casizolu
Casu Becciu
Casu Iscaldidu
Casu Marzu
Dolce Sardo
Fiore Sardo
Fresa
Moro del Logudoro
Pecorino Romano
Pecorino Sardo

Pecorino Toscano
Ricotta Moliterna

Sicily
Burrini
Canestrato
Incanestrato
Pecorino Canestrato
Pecorino Siciliano
Piacentino
Piacentinu Ennese
Primo Sale
Ragusano
Ricotta Salata
Vastedda della Valle del Belìce

Trentino-Alto Adige
Asiago
Asiago d'Allevo
Asiago Grasso Monte
Asiago Pressato
Fontal
Grana Padano
Provolone Valpadana
Puzzone di Moena
Spressa delle Giudicarie
Stelvio
Vezzena

Tuscany
Caciotta Altopascio
Caciotta di Siena
Pastorella del Cerreto di Sorano
Pecorino delle Balze Volterrane
Pecorino Romano
Pecorino Senese
Pecorino Toscano

Umbria
Caciotta al Tartufo
Caciotta Norcia

Valle d'Aosta
Aostino
Fontina
Fontina d'Aosta
Fontini
Toma
Valle d'Aosta Fromadzo

Veneto
Asiago
Asiago d'Allevo
Asiago Grasso Monte
Asiago Pressato
Casatella Trevigiana

Crescenza
Grana Padano
Montasio
Monte Veronese
Morlacco
Piave
Pressato
Provolone Valpadana
Taleggio

Many Regions
Bocconi Giganti
Caciotta
Caprini
Fior di Latte
Formaggelle
Giuncata
Grana
Pecorino
Provola
Provolone
Raviggiolo
Ricotta
Ricotta Salata
Scamorza

APPENDIX C

Grapes: The Wines They Make

Name of Grape/ Color/ Dry–Sweet	Wines Made From This Grape
Aglianico (Red) Dry	Aglianico, Taurasi
Barbera (Red) Dry	Barbera; used a blending grape in many wines
Brachetto (Red) Semisweet to Sweet	Brachetto
Cabernet Sauvignon (Red) Dry	Bordeaux–Graves, Médoc, Pomerol, Saint-Émilion
Chardonnay (White) Dry	French Burgundy–Chablis, Mâcon-Villages, Mercurey, Pouilly-Fuissé, Saint-Véran; French Champagne
Chenin Blanc (White) Dry to Sweet and even Sparkling	Loire–Bonnezeaux, Chinon, Coteaux du Layon, Montlouis, Quarts de Chaume, Saumur, Savennières, Vouvray; South Africa–Steen
Cortese (White) Dry	Gavi
Corvina (Red) Dry	Amarone della Valpolicella, Bardolino, Valpolicella, Ripasso
Dolcetto (Red) Dry	Dolcetto
Fiano (White) Dry	Fiano, Fiano di Avellino
Friulano (White) Dry	Friulano
Fumé Blanc (White) Dry	Sauvignon Blanc
Gamay (Red) Dry	Beaujolais
Gewürztraminer (White) Dry to Sweet	Gewürztraminer, Traminer Aromatico

Greco (White) Dry	Greco di Ancona, Greco di Bianco, Greco di Todi, Greco di Tufo
Grenache (Red) Dry	Italy–Cannonau; France–Rhône–Châteauneuf-du-Pape, Côtes-du-Lubéron, Côtes-du-Rhône, Côtes-du-Ventoux, Gigondas, Lirac, Vacqueyras; Tavel
Grignolino (Red) Dry	Grignolino
Lambrusco (Red) Dry to Semisweet	Lambrusco
Malbec (Red) Dry	Bordeaux–Graves, Médoc, Pomerol, Saint-Émilion
Merlot (Red) Dry	Bordeaux–Graves, Médoc, Pomerol, Saint-Émilion
Montepulciano (Red) Dry	Montepulciano d'Abruzzo; used a blending grape in many wines
Muscat (White) Dry to Sweet and even Sparkling	Italy—Asti, Moscato; France—Muscat de Beaumes-de-Venise, Muscat de Frontignan; South Africa—Constantia; Portugal—Moscatel de Setúbal
Nebbiolo (Red) Dry	Barbaresco, Barolo, Carema, Donnas, Gattinara, Ghemme, Grumello, Inferno, Roero Rosso, Sassella, Sforzato, Spanna, Valgella
Palomino Fino (White) Dry	Sherry
Petit Verdot (Red) Dry	Bordeaux
Petite Sirah (Red) Dry	Petite Sirah
Picolit (White) Semisweet to Sweet	Picolit
Pinot Bianco (White) Dry	Pinot Bianco/ Pinot Blanc
Pinot Grigio (White) Dry	Pinot Grigio/ Pinot Gris
Pinot Meunier (Red) Dry	French Champagne
Pinot Noir (Red) Dry	French Burgundy; French Champagne; Dôle, Mercurey, Reuilly
Primitivo (Red) Dry	Primitivo
Prosecco (white) Semidry to Dry	Prosecco
Riesling (White) Dry to Sweet	Mosel, Rhine
Sagrantino (Red) Dry	Montefalco Sagrantino

Sangiovese (Red) Dry	Brunello di Montalcino, Carmignano, Chianti, Morellino di Scansano, Rosso Cònero, Rosso di Montalcino, Rosso di Montepulciano, Vino Nobile di Montepulciano
Sauvignon Blanc (White) Dry to Sweet	Bordeaux–Graves, Sauternes (Barsac); Fumé Blanc, Ménétou-Salon, Pouilly Fumé, Quincy, Reuilly, Sancerre
Syrah (Red) Dry	Rhône–Châteauneuf-du-Pape, Cornas, Côtes-du-Lubéron, Côtes-du-Rhône, Côtes-du-Ventoux, Côte Rôtie, Crozes-Hermitage, Gigondas, Hermitage, Lirac, Saint-Joseph, Vacqueyras: Shiraz
Trebbiano (White) Dry	Trebbiano, Trebbiano d'Abruzzo; used a blending grape in many wines
Verdicchio (White) Dry	Verdicchio
Zinfandel (Red or White) Dry to semisweet	Zinfandel

Other Wines & Beverages

Name of Beverage/ Color	Designations/Types/Styles/Base Ingredients
Beer (Dark-Colored)	Bock, Porter, Stout
Beer (Light-Amber Colored)	Ale, Lager, Pilsner, Wheat
Bourbon (Amber)—United States	Corn—rye, barley, wheat
Brandy (Fruit)	Calvados, Framboise, Fraise, Kirsch, Poire
Brandy (Grapes)	France–Armagnac, Cognac; Other Countries–California, Italy, Portugal, Spain
Frascati (White)–Italy	Dry
Grappa (Clear)	Made from Pomace (unaged brandy)
Madeira (Portugal)–Dry	Sercial, Rainwater, Verdelho
Madeira (Portugal)–Semisweet-Sweet	Boal, Malmsey
Marsala (Italy)	Dry or Sweet
Orvieto (White)–Italy	Dry
Port (Portugal)–Semisweet–Sweet	Ruby, Tawny, LBV (Late-Bottled-Vintage), Vintage
Rosé (Dry)	France–Anjou, Lirac, Provence, Tavel; Greece–Kokkinéli; Spain–Tempranillo; Or a rosé from virtually any other country
Rum (Clear-Amber, Dark)	Sugarcane
Scotch Whisky (Amber)–Scotland	Malted Barley-Based and Smoked
Sherry (Spain)–Dry	Manzanilla, Fino, Amontillado
Sherry (Spain)–Semisweet-Sweet	Oloroso, Cream, Brown, Pedro Ximénez
Soave (White)–Italy	Dry

Sparkling Wine & Champagne (Dry)	Champagne–Brut, Blanc de Blancs, Blanc de Noirs; Franciacorta, Prosecco, Brut Spumante
Sparkling Wine (Sweet)	Asti; Brachetto d'Acqui
Sweet Wines (Red or White)	Muscat, Picolit, Recioto di Soave, Riesling (late-harvest), Spumante (Asti), Vin Santo
Tennessee Whiskey (Amber)	Corn-Based
Vermouth (Dry)	White
Vermouth (Sweet)	Red or White

APPENDIX D

Cheese & Fruit Pairing

Name of Cheese	Fruit
Asiago	Apples, cantaloupe, figs, mango, melons, nectarines, peaches, pears, pineapple, plums, strawberries
Bagozzo	Apples, cantaloupe, figs, mango, melons, nectarines, peaches, pears, pineapple, plums, strawberries
Bel Paese	Apples, bananas, dates, figs, honeydew melon, pears, pineapple, strawberries
Blue or Blue-Veined Cheese	Apples, cherries, figs, grapefruit, honeydew melon, kumquats, melons, oranges, papaya, peaches, pears, pineapple, plums, raspberries, strawberries, and walnuts
Caciocavallo	Apples, figs, honeydew melon, pineapple
Crotonese	Apples, cantaloupe, figs, mango, melons, nectarines, peaches, pears, pineapple, plums, strawberries
Fiore Sardo	Melons, peaches
Fontina	Apples, cantaloupe, dates, figs, honeydew melon, nectarines, pears, pineapple, plums, raspberries, strawberries
Gorgonzola	Apples, banana, cantaloupe, honeydew melon, nectarines, oranges, papaya, peaches, pears, pineapple, plums
Grana Padano	Apples, cantaloupe, figs, mango, melons, nectarines, peaches, pears, pineapple, plums, strawberries
Mascarpone	Apples, bananas, blackberries, blueberries, cherries, currants, dates, figs, nectarines, oranges, papaya, peaches, pears, plums, quince, raspberries, strawberries
Mozzarella	Apples, melons, oranges, peaches, pineapple

Parmigiano-Reggiano	Apples, cantaloupe, figs, mango, melons, nectarines, peaches, pears, pineapple, plums, strawberries
Pecorino	Apples, cantaloupe, figs, mango, melons, nectarines, peaches, pears, pineapple, plums, strawberries
Provolone	Apples, cantaloupe, figs, honeydew melon, musk melon, Bartlett pears, pineapple, plums
Robiola	Nectarines, peaches, plums
Taleggio	Cherries, kumquats, melon, plums, watermelon
Triple-Crèmes	Apples, bananas, blackberries, blueberries, cherries, currants, dates, figs, nectarines, oranges, papaya, peaches, pears, plums, quince, raspberries, strawberries

Glossary

Affumicato: Smoked.

Bufala: Buffalo.

Cacio: An ancient Tuscan word for cheese.

Capra: Goat; the milk that is used to make cheese.

Caprino: Term for cheese made from goat's milk.

Caseificio: A dairy where cheese is made.

Duro: <u>Hard</u>. A descriptive term for cooked cheeses.

Formaggio: The term for Cheese.

Fresco: <u>Fresh</u>. A classification of cheese that does not undergo a ripening period before they are served. An example is Ricotta.

Giovane: Young.

Grana: A family of Italian cheeses that are granular, sharp, very well aged, and very hard. The Etruscans were probably the first to develop a cheese that could travel; for it was they who developed the hard-rind, long-aged cheese that we now call the *grana* type, which includes *Parmigiano-Reggiano* and *Pecorino*. See Grainy and Hard-Grating.

Grainy: A term used for describing a gritty texture, desirable in certain hard grating cheeses. Unless it is typical of the cheese, graininess is an undesirable trait. The opposite of grainy is "creamy."

Hard-Grating: A term used to classify cheeses that are salted, well-aged, and are easily grated.

Molle: <u>Soft</u>. Unpressed, high moisture mildly aged cheese.

Pasta Filata: A technique developed by the Italians, which literally means, "spun paste." It refers to those stretched or "plastic curd" cheeses such as Mozzarella and Caciocavallo. The cheese is generally covered with hot whey, then kneaded or spun in long threads until it is transformed into a soft and pliable ball suitable for shaping. The final cheese can be hard or soft.

Pecora: Sheep; the milk that is used to make cheese.

Pecorino: The term for cheese made from sheep's milk.

Piccante: <u>Piquant</u>. A descriptive term for a sharp tasting cheese.

Stravecchio: Very Old.

Vacca: Cow; the milk that is used to make cheese.

Vacchino: The term for cheese made from cow's milk.

Vecchio: Old.

BOB LIPINSKI

Bob Lipinski, a Certified Sommelier, is the author of nine books and more than 500 articles. As a professional speaker, entertainer, and educator, he has conducted seminars worldwide. He has presented to businesses, Fortune 500 corporations, trade shows, and conventions. Bob taught the Executive Staff at The White House "How-To Pair Wine with Food," "Proper Wine Service," and "Sensory Evaluation Skills." He also has television and radio experience as a host, writer, and guest. Bob has held executive-level sales, training, and education positions in the Wine & Spirits Industry as well as a College Professor of Management & Marketing at N.Y. Institute of Technology; Visiting Professor at the Culinary Institute of America; and Dean of U.S. and International Studies at the Epicurean Institute of Italy. Bob has also worked as a consulting *enologist* and *viticulturist*.

GARY GRUNNER

Gary Grunner is the founder and managing partner of *Grapes On The Go, Inc.*, "A Cutting Edge Beverage Marketing Management Group." He is a 25-year veteran in the wine and spirits industry and has been fortunate to have worked with some of today's most successful importers and distributors in the wine business. His philosophy is very simple—"out of the box thinking, detailed customer service, utilize today's cutting edge technology, and partner with other top industry people in the field to deliver a successful program to his clients." Born and raised in New York, he is the first to say his Italian wine career started in 1982, when he spent a semester in Italy as a college student where he fell in love with Italian wines, Italian culture, discovered regional Italian cuisine, and the Italian "zest" for life.

In 2009, Gary was the Silver Award recipient of The Italian Trade Commission Distinguished Service Award for the work he has done promoting, educating, and building Italian wines in the United States.

Blog: www.grunneronwine.com Twitter: @grunneron wine.com

Made in the USA
Middletown, DE
27 March 2017